THE LEGAL EXTORTION RACKET

The law is the servant of the people, not its master.

Jim Diamond

UK COSTS LAWYER OF THE YEAR 2016, 2017, 2018 and 2020

Grosvenor House
Publishing Limited

This book is published by
Grosvenor House Publishing Ltd
Link House
140 The Broadway, Tolworth, Surrey, KT6 7HT.
www.grosvenorhousepublishing.co.uk

A CIP record for this book
is available from the British Library

ISBN 978-1-80381-330-1

Dedication

This book is dedicated to Becca, Adam, Bella and Harry,

my four children and Harry and Harper, my beautiful grandchildren.

To quote from the Nat King Cole song -*Nature Boy*:

"The greatest thing we ever learn is to love and be loved in return".

Contents

BIO-

I am approaching the end of a career in law spanning more than 40 years. During that period, I worked as an outdoor clerk for Weightman's, a small legal firm in Liverpool, at the end of the 1970s and moved to London in the early 1980s. I worked in-house for Clifford Turner (now Clifford Chance) during the 1980s and Allen & Overy during the 1990s. With Clifford Turner and Allen & Overy being two of the top five City of London law firms, I spent most of my time working on some of the highest legal costs, disputes, and budgets over a two-decade period.

Throughout the last two decades, I have worked independently. My client base has ranged from individuals and small and medium-sized enterprises (SMEs) to billionaires and corporate clients such as Goldman Sachs.

I have worked on many legal costs dispute cases throughout the UK. The different systems across England, Wales, Scotland and the Channel Islands all suffer, in my view, the same problems, including a lack of transparency and a lack of regulatory controls and protocols in protecting the client from overcharging.

My practical work on legal budgets can be traced back to my Clifford Turner days in the 1980s, which included collating a detailed budget on the property and banking legal costs for the Canary Wharf development.

As a costs team, we would meet on Monday mornings to discuss the cases and transactions the firm was working on or had pitched for. During my first month there, I nearly fell off my chair at the numbers mentioned when a takeover of rival retail giants was discussed. A £500 million transaction in those days was a lot of money!

In 1998, Legal 500 published my first article on hourly rates and defective billing practices. This article graphically showed the sort of billing irregularities used by most city law firms in the 1990s.

I have advocated for formal and accurate legal costs information/ budgets since the late 1990s. In 1999, I drafted another article published in Legal 500 on budget-based billing. I believe this to be the first article ever published on this subject.

By 2003, my reputation was in this field; I was asked to speak at the annual Law Society of England and Wales conference. A further request followed in 2005 for me to be a speaker at the Judges and Costs Judges Forum at the Royal Courts of Justice. I was, I believe, the first law cost person to be invited to these internal Judicial conferences.

I also sat on a panel at the Commercial Litigation Association's (CLAN) Annual Conference in 2009, when Lord Justice Jackson was the main speaker making his first public address on his planned overhaul of the civil justice system.

My presentation in front of the 100 or so delegates, the great and good of the commercial legal world, was on formulating various forms of budgets in big-ticket commercial cases. I believe I shocked Lord Justice Jackson with my first question at the presentation's start: 'Can we confirm how many delegates have ever actually prepared a budget?' This is a fundamental requirement of the professional conduct rules for solicitors, with the regulations on this issue having been introduced as far back as 1991. The show of hands was quite telling; just three or four of the delegates, over 95%, had not.

In 2010 the Legal Service Board (LSB), whose remit is to oversee the entire legal marketplace in England and Wales, did not even know what hourly rates top law firms were charging clients.

How do I know this extraordinary fact? In October 2010, I gave the LSB's legal team a seminar about costs, budget, billing irregularities and hourly rates. I specifically stated my concerns about billing practices and suggested a further talk on this subject. They never invited me back!

In 2012, two years after my seminar, the LSB produced a detailed report on the legal marketplace and referred to large corporate solicitor firms' hourly rates. The numbers they included were based entirely on the research I had conducted and published over the previous decade on this subject.

I was approached in 2013 by the Law Society of England and Wales to write the Tool Kit on Costs Management. 2013 was a watershed year in civil litigation as it saw the introduction of Lord Justice Jackson's cost reforms, with a fundamental part of his reform being cost management in the civil legal system. The Law Society of England and Wales published the tool kit to aid small member law firms during this transformation.

In October 2016, I received an unsolicited email from Deutsche Bank's Director of Global Procurement, New York office, which said:

"I've read multiple articles about you and your analysis of legal spending. I was hoping you would send me copies of your Client Guide to Controlling Legal Costs and The Price of Law".

We are generally interested in better understanding market rates. We have a large panel and many firms' rates, but we don't know how we really match the marketplace.

My statistics and numerous articles were sent to him. Over the following six months, I heard nothing from him, not even the courtesy of a reply.

The following year the *In-House Lawyer* (IHL) drafted an article titled Whose Dime? (McGregor, 2017) which included the following quote:

Deutsche Bank had notified pitching firms of its unwillingness to pay for trainees and newly qualified lawyers during its last adviser review, sending a jolt through the UK legal market. The practice of writing off the time of junior lawyers has been common for years in the US, reflecting in part higher relative salaries, charge-out rates and a propensity to clock up more tangential work as billable hours stateside.

Although I am sure this had nothing to do with me supplying them with my data and statistics, a reply to say thanks would have been excellent.

The IHL had also approached me before the article's publication for comment. Another quote from the same article was:

Legal costs specialist Jim Diamond has been perhaps the most vocal critic of billing practices, with his research arguing that Magic Circle firms have dramatically raised their benchmark rates over the last decade to exceed £1000 an hour often.

Diamond comments: "They've got away with murder. They've got away with continuously expanding their rate over the last 15 years and they've got away with very limited transparency. I am the ghost of Christmas future. I've been warning the city firms for years about hitting crash load, and now it's going to happen. Clients are not going to pay for it."

Diamond notes that Deutsche requested copies of his research on structuring legal costs in the middle of 2016, adding: "They're not stupid. When you pay £800 an hour for a partner, you do not want to be paying newly-qualified lawyers £350–£400 an hour. Who would in their right mind?"

Let me put some of this into context. In 2016, top hourly rates broke the £1000 mark. In 2021 a junior barristers' brief fee on a case I compiled a budget for was estimated to be more than £1 million. By 2020–2021 the top 100 law firms generated £27.7 billion in turnover (The Lawyer, 2021).

The legal system for commercial legal fees is at breaking point. In 2016, the Competition and Marketing Authority conducted in-depth research into the prices of the legal industry and recommended a greater need for transparency, including the publication of hourly rates/prices on law firms' websites. However, some six years later, none of the top law firms publish this information on their own websites.

This is not a law book and will not, I am sure, be easy reading for the UK legal industry.

I leave the last words from an article in The Guardian in September 2011 (Greenslade, 2011):

Cost lawyer Jim Diamond is determined to show that the system is iniquitous, arguing that major City law firms are guilty of massive over-charging. His latest assault can be found on the Legal Week website in an article headlined "How law lost its soul–the epidemic of overcharging clients by city law firms".

Introduction

My first job was delivering coal for a fella called Jimmy Diamond when I was 13. I would go on the truck and the swine would send me off carrying sacks of coal on my shoulders, and if it was raining, it was murder. I was paid nothing. When we needed coal, I'd say: "Can I take some of this?"

He said: "All right."

Gerry Marsden (Gerry and the Pacemakers)

(Wright, 2020)

I was born in Liverpool in the 1960s. There were eight of us living for my first 10 years in a three-bed terraced. One of my earliest memories is sharing a small bedroom with my three elder sisters.

My dad, Jimmy Diamond, was a hard, unforgiving man born in the Dingle, a very tough part of the city, in the 1930s. He worked 'on the coal' from the age of about 14 years of age, delivering door-to-door from the back of a horse-drawn cart.

As if by a rite of passage, when I was 15 years old, I also worked on the coal during my school holidays. The bags weighed approximately 100 weights (112lbs or nearly 51 kilos) and were delivered to houses and tenements in the docklands and housing estates of South Liverpool. It was back-breaking, dirty work. The coal dust inhaled would take ages to clear from your lungs, especially in the summer.

The winter had other added issues, not least an extra 5–10lbs per bag when they were wet and covered in ice.

I remember one December morning, two days before Christmas. The wind was howling off the Irish sea, and it was freezing. My first deliveries were in Garston, an area in South Liverpool covering the docklands. Ice was covering all the bags, and I wasn't wearing gloves, as you couldn't grab hold of the bags if you were wearing them. I started doing my deliveries, and within an hour, I'd had the skin removed from the top of two of my fingertips. Dad passed when he was 50, the accumulation of 30 years 'on the coal'.

I doubt that 95% of the lawyers who have constantly told me over the years how hard they are working would complete even one day doing this kind of work.

In the 1970s, Friday was payday in Liverpool, and wages were paid almost exclusively in cash. This meant the money for the delivered bags of coal had to be collected door-to-door on a Friday evening. Collecting between £2–£10 from about 75 customers meant that by the end of the night, the collector would be carrying about £500 in cash (several thousand pounds in today's money). Walking around with that much money could be risky in those areas and especially in the dark of the winter nights.

When I was about 12, I can remember helping my dad with the collection of money.

In 1978, I passed my driving test. That year I was given the job (without debate) of collecting the coal money by myself for the whole of that winter. The three vital elements I needed for the work were the customer book (a list of customer names and addresses and how much they owed), the car keys and a truncheon (my favourite was one from the 1950s, which had a metal rod inserted into the base and up to the middle of the shaft).

At the end of the 1970s, Liverpool reached record unemployment with figures of about 40% for those under 20s. The riots in the early 1980s resulted from the explosion of anger and social pressures. This was no game. The 'coal business' was an unforgiving tough working life.

Inner city education in the 1970s consisted of 40+ boys in a class, with teachers who could control us but, apart from one or two, never taught us anything above a basic education. My only meeting with a careers officer when I was about 13 lasted about 15 minutes, 10 minutes of which was spent talking about football. The one and only 'career' question I was asked was, 'Well, what factory do you want to work in?'

The teachers at our secondary school generally preferred the stick rather than the carrot method of teaching, corporal punishment being the norm. I remember one lesson when the entire class was caned because one of the boys had stuck two onions up his nostrils, and we all laughed. The kids' laughter resulted in this multi-corporal punishment, followed by the same teacher trying to teach us for the rest of the lesson. Don't worry, it never hurt or bothered us, but what a way to 'teach'.

When I was 15, I discovered weight lifting. The 'gym' was my mate's garage in Menlove Avenue, South Liverpool. He lived about 400 yards away from a house called 'Menlips'; although we never knew this at the time, fame was sprung upon this house in later years, as it was the house that John Lennon lived in with his auntie.

My trainer was my mate's dad, Mr Currie, who was one of the most influential people in my life. At 15, he taught us the self-respect of training and manners. Everyone who trained with him called him Mr Currie. He was a god-loving man who never complained, even though he had every right to. In his mid-30s, Mr Currie had an accident that made him wheelchair-bound for the rest of his life.

I went to Millbank College to do a night school class in Economics after I left school. Despite the teaching, I enjoyed it but did not have much of a clue about the subject. I do remember, though, that John Maynard Keynes and Milton Friedman, two of the leading economists of the 1920s, had fundamental differences in their theories. I failed the exam but discovered it was the teacher, not the subject, that counts.

The teacher, John Bateman, was in his first ever teaching role and truly inspired me to learn. Thirty-five years later, I received an unsolicited email from him as he was nearing retirement. He was in a reflective mood and asked if I had ever kept in touch with any of the others of his first-class members. Sadly, I had not. We exchanged pleasantries over a few emails. I thanked him for igniting my thirst for knowledge. In his last email to me, he wrote:

"You don't know this, but I used to get very depressed, worrying what would all become of you in Liverpool and the lack of prospects. I guess in your case, and I hope others, I need not have worried too much".

That's why I liked and respected him as a teacher; even back then, I could tell he cared.

Dad had told me there was no future in the family coal business, so by fluke; I found a job as an outdoor clerk at a small law firm in Liverpool in 1979. The four years there was an essential foundation for my future legal career. In 1983, I worked as a full-time legal costs clerk for a West End of London law firm.

Chapter 1
The Art of Legal Costs Budgeting

The legal sector is undoubtedly one of the UK's most significant financial industries. Within it, there is a millennium of experience and world renown. However, the two most important failures of the UK commercial legal world are the lack of transparency and the failure to supply detailed budgets on cases at an early stage of instructions and throughout the matter.

The vast majority of legal cost disputes I have been involved with between clients and their lawyers have contained some fundamental issues over the legal budget or cost-risk analysis.

The reason for this is unclear to me. Maybe it is simply a lack of training as there is very little time dedicated to this subject over the six or seven years spent studying to become a lawyer. Another reason, if one was cynical, maybe that law firms do not want to inform clients of the costs/risks of litigation as they may well lose out on that work.

The professional conduct rules clearly state that cost information should be given as early as possible and throughout the duration of the case/matter. A risk assessment should also be conducted, meaning the client must be aware of the risk against the reward of the legal work.

The recent spat between footballers' wives Coleen Rooney and Rebekah Vardy, which the newspapers dubbed the 'Wagatha Christie Case', started as an argument regarding an Instagram leak and ended up in litigation costing a considerable amount of money. Mrs Rooney described the £900,000 budget for Rebekah Vardy's costs as 'grotesque'. I wonder if they (Rooney and Vardy) were given legal costs risk assessments at the start of this litigation.

1

In cases where people were friends only for the friendship to end in litigation, emotions can sometimes overrule logic. You could tell a client that the legal cost could be in the region of £1 million, and they may not care until either cooler heads prevail, or they get the bill. I'm not saying they didn't get the risk assessment, but I wonder if they did.

Relating to the Brack v Brack [2020] EWHC 2142 (Fam) matrimonial case, in which the legal costs exceeded £2 million, Mr Justice Francis commented:

> *It would, I respectfully suggest, have been wiser to spend that money on each other and not on their excellent but expensive legal teams.*

I once compiled an in-depth and detailed legal budget for an offshore law firm on a complex trust matter. With the information I was given, I estimated the costs to be £250,000. How did I draw such a conclusion? Let me explain. I start by looking at the facts, the evidence, the quantum, the parties and the law firms involved and using any other salient points to formulate the basic template budget.

I produced the legal budget of the case running to a six-page excel spreadsheet. I presented my budget and reasoning at a meeting with the instructing partner. He sat quietly, sipping on his coffee while I went through everything. Once I had finished, he simply picked up the spreadsheet, ripped it up and put it in the bin. He looked at me and, without an ounce of shame, said, 'I am not giving those figures to my client because if I did, I might not get the case'. So that was that.

In 2012, I met with a city law firm on a case in which a US litigation funder instructed me to prepare a formal budget. At the meeting, we went through the process of case/budget. The partner said she thought the trial would last no more than 10–12 days. I disagreed and included eight weeks trial duration in the budget. As one can imagine, our difference would significantly impact the overall legal budget. Her view was that this was going to end up with only two or three major legal arguments but going on the information in front of me, a competition dispute involving tens of millions of pounds and over 20 Defendants was likely to be very expensive and run way more at trail than her suggestion.

My client wanted a costs budget based on a worst-case scenario. I met the client in Claridge's for tea. I suggested he order a gin and tonic (as he was going to need it) when I presented him with the budget. My figures came out at £35 million. He then ordered a double gin and tonic, immediately called the lawyer, and a heated argument ensued.

My words of wisdom are that if a law firm is reluctant to give a detailed budget, I would be as reluctant to use them for their services.

Chapter 2
String Theory-

In August 2021, the Association of Costs Lawyers (ACL) published an article titled 'String Theory' that I had written about the SKAT litigation case.

In this case, Acupay System LLC v Stephenson Harwood LLP [2021] EWHC B11 (Costs), Master Leonard gave a complete and detailed judgment on the fundamental issues of this matter surrounding the conditional fee agreement (CFA) between the client Acupay and its former solicitors, Stephenson Harwood.

By way of background, I was instructed by Acupay in May 2020 to produce budgets for two variations, one for a split trial of approximately three weeks and one for the possibility of a 50-week trial.

My retained work concluded with the production of the two budgets. I had no dealings in the Solicitors Act proceedings.

"Thumb in the air."

I have worked in commercial legal costs budgeting since the 1980s. However, my experience has always been a massive reluctance to produce detailed budgeting for commercial cases.

The standard lawyer response to a client requesting a budget – 'How long is a piece of string?' – has been replaced recently by a client of mine being asked if he wanted a thumb in the air budget'.

Acupay was one of more than 100 Defendants in proceedings brought by SKAT, the Danish customs and tax administration, which claimed to have been induced by misrepresentations to pay out over £1.5 billion as tax refunds it was not liable for.

The case, which was scheduled to last for the whole of 2023 and was likely to become the costliest commercial court trial ever, was struck out in April when Mr Justice Andrew Baker ruled SKAT was trying to enforce Danish revenue law overseas, in a way that was not admissible in the English courts. At that point, the various Defendants had 21 separate legal teams from 18 firms of solicitors.

Once instructed directly by the client, I set up several Zoom calls with the legal team and looked at the core paperwork. The largest of the two budgets I drafted came out at £19.7 million. This budget was presented to Mr Justice Andrew Baker at a case and costs management conference in July 2020. Subsequently, that budget figure formed the basis of the Defendants seeking the security of costs against SKAT in the £600 million bracket.

My concerns

In a section of Master Leonard's judgment on estimates, he noted:

The Claimant has instructed a Costs Lawyer to prepare costs budgets for a full 50-week trial, as opposed to a three-week trial for the non-fraud Defendants and complains that the Defendant's approach would cost them an additional £17m, along with the advantages attendant on a deferring cost for several years. Mr Lambersy [president of the Claimant] says that the Claimant could not afford a 50-week trial. Had he been properly advised at the time with this sort of detailed cost information, he says, he would have accepted SKAT's proposal.

Master Leonard also referred to the professional conduct rules on budgets:

I appreciate that professional standards require that a solicitor managing a contentious business provide a client with the best possible information on present and future costs continuingly. As far as I can see, Defendant, which in January 2019 produced a quite comprehensive estimate of costs for the coming year (and, to some extent, beyond), did as much as one could reasonably expect at that stage to forecast the future costs of litigation that, by its nature, was replete with uncertainties.

The Solicitors Regulation Authority (SRA) code of conduct requires solicitors to:

Ensure that clients receive the best possible information about how their matter will be priced and, both at the time of engagement and when appropriate as their matter progresses, about the likely overall cost of the matter and any costs incurred.

In his ruling, Master Leonard seemed to accept that it is only necessary for a budget to cover a limited period, rather than the whole case, to satisfy these rules. He also did not comment on any potential adverse costs budget, which should, in my view, always be formulated for the benefit of a client.

I am concerned about whether this is the Senior Courts Costs Office's future interpretation of the professional conduct rules. A formal budget should be produced as early as possible, and an adverse costs budget should also be made to understand the risk better and reward basis of litigation and the client's ability to fund and seek funding or insurance.

Dismissive attitude

Of course, I cannot say how accurate my budget estimate of £19.7 million would have been. A budget for a case of this type should always be viewed as an organic document and reviewed at least quarterly.

I can say that the day after the case was struck out, I was interviewed live on Danish TV and asked about the likely cost consequences to the Danish taxpayer. I suggested SKAT face an interim payment of £50 million. The following month, Andrew Baker J ordered interim costs of £46.6 million.

Let that sink in. I had not worked on the case for nearly a year and only for one of the numerous Defendants, but I could still estimate the figures accurately. I am not bragging, it's my job, but it just leaves me appalled that the legal profession remains so fundamentally against and dismissive of legal budgets.

I never hope to see another file referring to lengths of string or fingers in the air.

Update September 2021

I wrote to the senior costs judge questioning the judgement and, more specifically, to ask whether the judiciary had any guidelines as this judgment had possible consequences for big-ticket litigation cases. His written response was simply, 'No Comment!'

BACKGROUND

I found it disappointing from a professional perspective that Master Leonard did not mention my name in his judgment but simply referred to a costs lawyer who had produced the budget.

On 6th April 2020, Master Leonard, on another case in which a potential client enquired about retaining my services, e-mailed him and cc the other parties in the litigation stating:

"*I can understand Mr X's wish to be represented. I think he must be misinformed about Mr Diamond's medical condition, as a quick internet search against Mr Diamond's name indicates he is posting on Twitter. There is no mention of illness and a picture posted 4th April 2020 indicates he is quite well*"

Column Leonard

Costs Judge.

Twitter, TWITTER! I am still lost for words that a Judge could do this. What a sad reflection of the judiciary in 2020's.

Chapter 3
The 'Onion Man Case'

My first job in London was with a law firm named Baileys Shaw and Gillett (BSG) in 1983. My interview for the job happened the week before I started and was conducted by the manager, who had been with the firm since the early 1960s.

I say interview, but in reality, we spent more time discussing football than we did discuss my previous four years' experience at Weightman's, a Liverpool law firm that at the time I left had only one office and 12 employees but is now a top 45 UK law firm with over 1300 employees and offices in eight cities including London. After the interview, the manager took me to lunch at the Star Cafe, a famous eatery in the W1 area.

I started work at BSG on 4 July 1983, my Independence Day. I had never been to university, so this was my first experience living alone and away from Liverpool.

The firm was located at 5 Berners Street, which ran from Wardour Street across Oxford Street into the centre of the shopping area, restaurants and pubs, so I was in the midst of everything. It seemed like the centre of the world at times.

The building itself was an old Edwardian house which wasn't very wide but was seven stories high with plenty of character. The partners were situated at the front of the offices overlooking Berners Street, while the rest were at the back of the building.

I worked in a small (about 16ft x 16ft) office containing dark shelves filled with old accounts. There were files all over the floor, and the smell of smoke lingered in the air, as in those days, you could smoke in the workplace, and my manager was a heavy smoker.

At that time, 18 partners and 75 staff were working at BSG. The managing partner of BSG was a wonderful man. The dictionary defines a gentleman as a chivalrous, courteous, or honourable man. This was a perfect description of Mr Bishop. He simply had a way about him like a headmaster, lawyer and captain of a ship all rolled into one. A genuine and humble man who would treat everyone, from the firm's top clients to the office messenger, with the same level of respect.

I remember him one day giving me a pep talk on the importance of the job that I was doing. He told me that while the clients rarely read much of the paperwork solicitors send them, they always check their bills.

He said, 'Jim, I could write a 50-page document, and the client would only really be concerned about whether the bill and covering letter they had received had a correct address and post code'. A wise man was Mr Bishop!

My two years at BSG as a full-time cost clerk were a fabulous experience for me both in terms of learning the nuances of the commercial legal cost field and my personal growth as a country boy arriving in the metropolis.

There are many remarkable stories about my time at BSG; way too many to write about in this book. However, I suppose if I had to choose, the one I remember fondest involved Mr Bishop and the backroom boys.

My memory is a bit hazy, but I think this incident occurred at the end of the first billing month. I was the only one in the office because the backroom boys had gone out for a late lunch. In the 1980s, late lunches involved pub food and alcohol, although sometimes alcohol was the only thing on the menu.

I was the new boy at the firm, so I had to stay behind and run the office. Before they left, the backroom boys gave me strict instructions: if any senior partners needed them, I was to say they were in a meeting.

Around 2.30 pm, the phone rang. It was Mr Bishop's secretary who said he needed some financial information right away. I told her about the meeting as instructed and promised to let them know ASAP.

About an hour later, the phone rang again. It was the secretary. Under considerable pressure, she insisted I get someone to retrieve the information and bring it to her, NOW!

I knew then that I had to track down the boys or else there would be hell to pay. I decided to speak to a senior accounts lady called Margaret. I thought it would be her if anyone knew where they might be. After I told Margaret my predicament, she just laughed, told me to relax and directed me to a bar called the Dolls House, which was found in Soho just around the corner from the Star Cafe.

I quickly thanked her and took off in the direction of Soho to find my colleagues. Now you must understand that I knew next to nothing about Soho at this particular time. In the 1970s and early 1980s, Soho had a very sleazy reputation. It was inhabited by prostitutes, strip clubs, and the type of people who used their services.

Being new to the area, I thought the Doll's House would simply be a W1 wine bar. I was going to rush in, let the boys know what was happening then hightail it back to work. It took me about five minutes to walk from the office to the 'wine bar', and the moment I arrived at my destination, the penny dropped. I was greeted by a building covered with what I can only describe as pretty artistic photographs of ladies with little to no clothes on and two large bouncers.

As I approached the building, I noticed a sign that said there was a £10 entry fee which I didn't want to pay as I was just going in to deliver a message, so I walked up to the bouncers and said in my thick Liverpudlian accent said, 'I don't want to go in, but do you know if my bosses are in there?' Nothing! No response. They thought I was trying it on.

I didn't want to fork out £10 just to go into the 'bar' for two or three minutes, but the alternative was to go back to the office and tell the senior partners that the whole of the finance team was at a strip club.

The New Millennium legal generation will never face such a dilemma. One of the things I learned very early on in my career was diplomacy. Sort out the problem first and then deal with the consequences later.

So, I paid the £10 and then had to go through the process of leaving my details with the membership secretary.

I very quickly found what I had come for. The team took up the first two rows of seats, drinking, laughing and having a good time. I hurried over to them and explained what was happening back at the office while the stage act was fully flowing. To this day, I'm unsure who was peed off the most, at the interruption, my colleagues for interrupting their enjoyment or the lady on the stage with hardly any clothes on trying to earn a living. We returned to the office at 4 pm; the partner received the information by 4.30 pm, and the backroom boys were back at the Doll's House by 5 pm.

My primary function at BSG and any cost clerk in the 1980s was to quantify the legal costs of a matter or case and then draft a bill for the client. Most commercial law firms had an in-house costs clerk in their employ. The old joke about a lawyer weighing a file and the heavier the file, the larger the bill was not too far from the truth.

Very few law firms in the early-mid 80s had any time recording system. The job of a cost clerk, therefore, was to count letters, telephone calls, court hearings and client appointments, and also to review work done on the general preparation of the case from a combination of the case file, the job done and the solicitor's diary.

Once all the information was gathered, the clerk would have to put all the entries together, draft a narrative of the work and bill the client. What could therefore go wrong with such a forensic account exercise?

The 'Onion Man Case'

In 1982, one of the most notorious cases of overbilling from the 1970s was finally adjudicated. I did not work on the case, but I knew a cost clerk who did, so I have some idea about what happened. The conclusion of the 'Onion Man case', which is what we called it, would send shock waves throughout the legal profession and have ramifications for the rest of the 1980s.

In the 1970s, Leslie Arthur Parsons allegedly invented a machine that could peel the top layer of onions quickly and cost-effectively. As you can imagine, a device of that nature could be worth millions of pounds, and the development would require substantial legal input. To that end, Mr Parsons hired a solicitor called Mr Glanville Davis. Glanville Davis and Parsons had a good working relationship over the years. The two spent considerable time together and became friends, which is common.

The relationship between Messrs Glanville Davis and Parsons took a downturn, and they had a significant falling out, ending their working relationship and friendship.

Mr Glanville Davis submitted a legal bill to Mr Parsons for his services totalling £198,000. By comparison, during the same period, an average house sold for just £19,273.

The issues escalated into a formal litigation dispute between the two men. Mr Glanville Davis produced a detailed account of the work he was claiming for. Whoever produced the breakdown made a massive mistake by claiming a full day's work with Mr Parsons. It turns out that the day claimed for was the day of the wedding of Mr Parson's daughter.

The Law Society rejected the complaint in 1978, so Mr Parsons had to pursue the case through the High Court.

I am not au fait with the details of the court proceedings, but after four years of litigation, the High Court found in favour of Mr Parsons and reduced Mr Glanville Davis's legal bill from the £198,000 claimed to £67,000, which is a reduction of more than 60%.

An application was made that Mr Granville Davis, admitted as a solicitor in 1945, be struck off the roll of solicitors of the Supreme Court. Mr Glanville Davis never opposed the application.

The case also brought into question the credibility of the England and Wales Law Society. They had rejected the claim four years earlier, stating that there was no case to investigate. The SRA now conduct these misconduct issues involving law firms and lawyers. Forty years later, the situation in my personal experience has not improved (see Chapter 4).

In the modern legal business, it is paramount that a law firm provides as much accurate and detailed information on the cost of its services to the client as possible. In almost all legal costs disputes I have dealt with over the last two decades, there has been some kind of disagreement over pertinent information either not being given, not being updated, or sadly being fundamentally flawed.

Over the years, I have been invited to speak at many internal legal costs seminars for law firms on legal budgets. I also make reference that a client who is unhappy with the bill could tie the law firm in Litigation/Regulatory dispute for months, if not years.

For small and medium-sized law firms, that action could lead to serious financial ramifications; in 2014, when The England and Wales Law Society invited me to give a short presentation at their Civil Costs Sections Annual Seminar about budgets at their offices on Chancery Lane. As part of my presentation, I spent £500 getting a proforma cash flow budget in a zip package. The budget contained monthly breakdowns and a variety of graphs and pie charts, budget and cashflow in one.

I informed the 94 delegates who had attended the seminar that they could all have a copy of my cash flow budget free with no restrictions and multiuser. Not one of the 94 delegates present accepted my offer.

Why? In my opinion, they were not interested in changing the status quo—a sad and troubling reflection of the legal profession in the 21st century.

Chapter 4
The 'Bottle of Wine Case'

In my 40+ years in the legal business, one of the most scandalous cases I have ever worked on involved a bottle of wine, a partner of a city London law firm substantially overcharging and the Solicitors Regulatory Authority ("SRA") conducting a seven-year investigation.

As in the 'Onion Man case' in Chapter 3, this case became known as the 'Bottle of Wine case' following a discovery I made while conducting my audit. Why that title? Keep reading, and all will be revealed.

In 2015, I was instructed by a client, Mr GK, to deal with a costs dispute involving his former London law firm. The case involved litigation in Jersey, and the London law firm was retained to manage the proceedings with Jersey Advocates and English counsel.

On 18 June 2014, the client travelled from Jersey to London for business purposes. Once he had arrived, he called partner Mr SA, and it was agreed that a quick meeting would be beneficial. While en route to the meeting, Mr GK received a message from Mr SA suggesting that they do not meet at his place of work but rather at the Emperor pub, which was about a mile from his firm's offices. That was not unusual; as I've said, this was more of a catch-up than a confidential legal meeting concerning the intricate details of the litigation: the client Mr SA and some of his colleagues who had been in the pub for a while. Since Mr GK had further business to attend to that evening, he left as soon as the discussion was over but not before picking up a £74.85 bar bill for a **bottle of wine.**

When the litigation was concluded, the client was presented with his bill, and that's when I was called in. I audited the working papers and discovered considerable discrepancies in the time recording system relating to Mr SA. These discrepancies included Mr SA recording vast chunks of time but not giving any details of the work that he had allegedly done.

Modern time recording systems allow solicitors/fee earners to log the time spent on the case and the ability to include a detailed narrative of the work done. This is of paramount importance as it helps law firms to confirm the job done and justify their fees, especially when the hourly rates are high.

Mr SA, at that time, was charging £400 an hour. So, to find hundreds of hours billed with zero narratives was of great concern.

During the audit process, I noted there was time logged on 18 June 2014 by Mr SA. I asked Mr GK about that day, and he recounted the above story. I informed him that Mr SA had recorded seven hours for that day. At £400 per hour, that equates to £2800, plus the £74.85 for the bottle of wine for a brief discussion on the case in a pub.

Mr GK assumed there must be some kind of error regarding the date. I informed him that Mr SA had also recorded exactly seven hrs of work on Monday 16th, Tuesday 17th, Thursday 19th and Friday 20th June. A total of 35 hrs, which is at £400 per hour, equates to £14,000 for the week.

I contacted the complaints partner at the law firm and concisely pointed out the multiple errors I had discovered. This led to a formal meeting in their offices in February 2015 with their in-house team. Mr SA surprisingly did not attend.

The role of the complaints partner is to deal with issues like billing objectively and to resolve these matters as quickly as possible. The meeting did not go well. With raised voices and a lack of empathy, the issues I raised were never considered or accepted. The law firm threatened to issue proceedings against my client if the bill was not paid in full.

Subsequently, a letter before action was issued against my client for the total outstanding amount to be paid within seven days of the meeting.

Neither I nor Mr GK was intimidated by these threats. There followed seven months of legal proceedings in the Supreme Court Costs office. The law firm utilises a legal team of five in-house lawyers and a barrister to justify their legal fees.

Two court hearings took place before one of the top Costs Judges, who answered my concerns about the possible potentially massive amount of time dumping with this statement:

'In my experience, lawyers are as likely to under record time as over record time".

I obtained a transcript of this hearing to show the Mr GK the difficulties of running this legal cost litigation. In this case, for example, the law firm ran up approximately £50,000 attempting to justify its legal bills. In October 2015, the law firm suggested mediation rather than costly litigation.

The mediation was held in December 2015, at the same offices as my first meeting, with the same law firm members in attendance and a £2500 a day mediator. The mediation concluded with the usual legal jargon of a non-disclosure agreement for both parties.

Let's just say the bill was not paid in full. To this day, Mr GK never received a breakdown of the hundreds of hours claimed by Mr SA nor an apology from the law firm or Mr SA himself.

The conduct issues with the SRA against partner Mr SA continued. I submitted my letter of complaint to the SRA on 3 March 2015. Mr SA left the law firm at the end of April 2015, some three months after my meeting with the complaints team.

The role of the SRA is to oversee and regulate more than 150,000 practising solicitors and 10,000 law firms across England and Wales. The duties of the members include setting the strategic direction at meetings, holding the executive to account for its performance, representing the views of a wide range of diverse external stakeholders and acting as ambassadors.

Below is an extract from the SRA 's website (SRA, 2019):

There are seven principles that all people and law firms we regulate must meet. This means that they must act:

In a way that upholds the constitutional principle of the rule of law, and the proper administration of justice

In a way that upholds public trust and confidence in the solicitors' profession and legal services provided by authorised persons

With independence

With honesty

With Integrity

In a way that encourages equality, diversity and inclusion

In the best interests of each client.

Although this extract makes for very impressive reading, it's just words.

The initial complaint to SRA was rejected with a standard cut-and-paste letter. I had assumed that considering my background experience and reputation in the legal profession, any individual who read my letter would have bothered to investigate the matter before dismissing it. I produced a 207-page witness statement in the costly litigation and sent it to the SRA to back up my initial detailed letter of complaint. The SRA lost this statement four times during the seven years of their investigation.

I appealed the initial dismissal of the complaint and suggested that the investigator read my witness statement in its entirety. I received requests from the SRA in 2016 to resend my witness statement on two occasions.

As the costs litigation concluded with the law firm at the end of 2015, I continue to act for Mr GK regarding the complaint proceedings against Mr SA on a pro bono basis. Such were my concerns about the overcharging.

I have a story to tell you. I was the co-founder of an amateur football club in 1991. In the first season, I don't think we won a game. In the second season, now as the appointed manager, we became champions of West London's Sunday league division two.

Halfway through the second season, we were becoming successful; we attracted more players, all wanting to play football every Sunday. The resulting disharmony among the team required me to call an emergency meeting.

Before the meeting, I sent out a 'blind' questionnaire to the team members, giving them a platform to speak freely about the football team's running.

About 90% of the questionnaires were sent back to me, and to be honest, I was expecting some criticism, but I was not prepared for shocking and wholly inappropriate comments.

I am not a gambler, but if I were, I would certainly not do so without 'marking the cards.

When I sent out the blind questionnaires, I marked the back page with individual numbers so I knew every player who had replied, and when I ended the meeting, I informed the players that I had marked their cards and knew who had said what. To this day, certain team members refuse to talk to me.

So why am I telling you this? When the SRA requested my statement for the third time, I submitted it, but I deliberately removed every third page of my 207-page statement. It was my way of knowing if they had read the document or not. I marked the cards!

My appeal was unsuccessful. The SRA stated that a further and complete investigation into the complaint had occurred, and there was no case to answer. I knew they had 't read my statement. If they had, they would have noted every 3rd page was missing from my statement.

After their outrageous conduct, I returned to the SRA and called in a senior investigator to oversee the appeal/complaint. I got the usual rubbish about the SRA being overworked and under-resourced. He confirmed the complaint would be given high priority in 2016. By high priority was that it took their external legal costs expert three years to produce a draft audit report of the billing issues I had raised in my complaint letter submitted to the SRA on 3rd March 2015.

The senior investigator left the SRA, and several other investigators dealt with this matter. In May 2019, a new investigator spent two days with the client and me in Jersey. He had minimal experience in dealing with this type of complaint. Half of our time was spent educating him on the process of commercial legal costs/Jersey litigation.

His primary function was to take a proof from the client and then produce a draft statement. Once our meeting concluded, I expected a turnaround of this statement within two weeks. It took 16 months and two further investigator changes before receiving the client's draft statement.

In August 2019, the SRA moved the matter out of their Birmingham office to their London office. A solicitor was appointed as the lead investigator. We met in August, and I updated her on the previous four years of the SRA's investigation and requested to know what progress would be made. After the meeting, the solicitor informed me that the SRA had again lost the exhibits to my witness statement.

Over the next year, other statements were prepared. Then to my dismay, in December 2020, the SRA wrote to the client directly to say they had mislaid the exhibits in his witness statement.

In December 2020, having made formal complaints against the SRA's handling of this matter, I was informed that due to partner Mr SA's personal situation, he had requested that the formal complaint letter not be served over Christmas. They granted his request and didn't serve him until January, giving him more time to prepare his response. Even more, time was afforded to him as the deadline was moved again, this time to March 2021, six years after my initial complaint.

In July 2019, I was given the independent costs audit report for my overall views. The SRA put an embargo on it, so I could not discuss the content during the proceedings, even with my client. The hundreds of hours of questionable time for Mr SA were picked up in the report. However, the information raised issues of the £400 per hour being charged too high. I specifically went back to them and said this was a dude point as my client, a sophisticated buyer of legal services, knew or should have known what the going hourly rates are/likely to be for London partners.

Towards the end of 2021, the SRA concluded that the matter did not have enough evidence to progress to a full SDT hearing due to the time delay and the hourly rate issue. After further correspondence, the file was closed in February 2022, just short of seven years after I lodged the first formal complaint.

There are approximately 150,000 solicitors, which the SRA have a remit to overview. I was informed that the SRA only employed six field investigators: ex-police officers or the like. I am sure they can deal with the run-of-the-mill complaints, but I must seriously question how, with no/limited experience, they can deal with more complex commercial legal costs issues.

The SRA receive something like 12,000 individual complaints a year, so over 80,000 complaints were made during the seven years of this complaint.

Complaining About the Conduct of the SRA in the 'Bottle of Wine Case'

The SRA have a complaints procedure to deal with issues regarding their service/conduct.

I started this process during the 5th year of the SRA investigation. The initial process goes through a two-tier internal complaints system within the SRA.

After this complete waste of time, the next step is a third complaint which the independent reviewer deals with at the centre for effective dispute resolution (CEDR).

This is done on paper; no further evidence or oral submissions are allowed. I lodged the formal complaint about the conduct of SRA with the CEDR in February 2021.

Issues raised in the complaint in brief:

SRA is Unfit for purpose on 'big ticket' legal costs issues/disputes.

The six-year delay in progressing the matter.

The reviewer's misconduct in saying they read all papers (as stated above, I deliberately omitted every third page of my 207-page witness statement).

The level of experience and number of the investigatory officers. In conclusion, it was something like ten people who worked on the complaint.

I recommend that SRA instruct/retain people with the necessary experience in big-ticket legal disputes/matters.

The response I received from the CEDR independent reviewer is outlined below:

As an independent reviewer, my remit is to consider the quality of service the SRA provides, including its complaints handling team.

Observations on the SRA letters and apologies by the SRA

I have carefully considered the exchange between yourself and the SRA, including but not limited to the information kindly provided by you and the SRA letters and other communications.

About your first complaint raised on 10 June 2020, the SRA, in its letter dated 22 June 2020, accepted that its record-keeping had been poor and caused you and the client considerable inconvenience and additional work and apologised for that poor service. It also stated their point in time; there were delays that should have been avoided.

Furthermore, regarding your first complaint in its letter on 6 August 2020, the SRA apologised that its service was not of the standard it hoped to provide and was in the process of making changes to the procedures initiated in 2015.

I note that in its letter of 6 August 2020, it offered a goodwill gesture of payment of £100 to both yourself and the client. The issue of such an ex-gratia offer has not been raised in your application and falls outside the remit of this review.

You have very helpfully summarised your areas of complaint concisely in your email dated 3 February 2021 as relating to delay, loss of documents, and lack of understanding of commercial cost/ procedures/rules regulations. I will address these issues in turn.

Overall delay

As mentioned above, the SRA has admitted that there were delays that should have been avoided. In its letter dated 22 June 2020, the SRA said it would expect an investigation of this complexity to take approximately two to three years to complete, working as we do on other matters.

In summary, the reasons given for exceptional circumstances were, in no particular order, changes in personnel, staff absence and illness, the complexity of the matter and the considerable amount of evidence to be gathered and analysed, and the time taken to complete an independent report by the duly elected and appointed costs draftsperson.

While the SRA has provided a detailed explanation in its letter dated 22 June 2020 as to the chronology regarding such delays, which is helpful, and admitted that there were delays that should have been avoided, I take the view that the SRA has taken too long to deal with this matter, with what appears to be, over 4.5 years to reach the stage of reviewing the evidence and serving a notice on partner 'S'.

As to changes in personnel, it is understandable that there would be changes in personnel over such a period, but there seems to have been a lack of clarity/ detail from the SRA as to when such changes took place at the time that they occurred.

As to staff absences and illnesses that seems to have been an inordinate amount of misfortunate befalling those dealings with this matter, I cannot criticise anyone for those circumstances save referring to my previous point to inform the complainant regarding any enforced or temporary staff.

As to the complexity of the matter and the considerable amount of evidence to be gathered and analysed regarding what is described as alleged time dumping, I appreciate that the investigation will have been complex and highly document heavy. However, based on the SRA'S express view of how long such an investigation of this nature takes on average, this investigation has taken up to twice as long as that average, which is unacceptable in my view.

Loss of Documents

As stated above, the SRA has acknowledged they fell short of providing a good service regarding retention, location and ready access to documents. You have referred to the repeated displacement of witness statements. The SRA has stated that its procedures are processes and that a new IT system should have been in place by the end of 2020. Bearing in mind the enforced changes in working practises with an emphasis on working remotely with secured access to documents and colleagues, this is an essential issue to a growth to address both specifically concerning this complaint and more generally.

Lack of Understanding of Commercial Costs/Procedure/Rules/ Regulations

I note that you are an extremely experienced expert in solicitors cost matters, which is undoubtedly a specialist and much demanded service.

The SRA has an extensive range of responsibilities and matters to consider and review, and in my opinion, cannot be expected to have a high level of expertise in all areas of inquiry that will be faced. At the same time, there were issues with the costs draftsperson, which as indicated I will address separately, SRA in my opinion, cannot be criticised for appointing an independent expert to assist them and the issue to address handle for the review is to on what basis the independent experts are retained and as to what level the SRA personnel should have knowledge and understanding of retail cost, which I'll address regarding any recommendations.

Conclusions and Recommendations

Based on my observations and the SRA's acknowledgement of any shortfall as to the service set out above, I make the following observations.

In my opinion, the delay of the SRA in dealing with this matter is unacceptable, and I note that the SRA has openly acknowledged this.

In my opinion, the manner in which the SRA has managed documentation in relation to this specific complaint was lacking and the SRA has indicated that it has changed its processes and IT systems since the outset of this matter in 2015.

In my opinion, while the delays caused by the appointed cost expert were outside the SRA's control, the SRA may wish in the context to review the way in which the SRA appoint and monitor independent experts.

I have as requested investigated your complaint within my remit and set out my conclusions above. This now finalises my review of this complaint and closes the matter.

The independent reviewer's report was submitted back to the SRA. I wrote directly to the CEO of the SRA about the matter. I was expecting some positive response, which I learnt was that my letter, and the findings of the CEDR report were referred to the team dealing with the complaint. So, the group within the SRA who had been seriously criticised in this report were then given it to react against its findings. To my knowledge, nothing has happened. No internal discipline, NOTHING!

Indeed, any reasonable person reading this farcical situation will be concerned about the effectiveness and professionalism of the SRA in dealing with legitimate complaints against law firms and lawyers. I wonder how many of the 80,000 people who made complaints during these seven years are aware of the SRA's failing procedures, as indicated in this case.

Finally, the client and I ignored the SRA's insulting gesture of ex-gratia payment of £100 each to cover the work/loss/frustrations dealing with the matter.

Chapter 5
The 'Golf Shoes Case' and Others

In an example of history repeating itself, 20 years after the infamous and highly publicised 'Onion Man case', there was the equally egregious case involving all things golf and a pair of golf shoes.

Unlike the 'Onion Man case', this was one of my own. Towards the end of the 1990s, I was retained by a client to audit the working papers on a case they had instructed with a now-defunct law firm in Manchester. The client had concerns about the bill's size on litigation that seemed to be out of control from a legal cost perspective.

During the litigation, the client held their annual corporate golf day. As in the 'Onion Man case, the client had formed a good relationship with their lawyer and decided to invite him to attend the event, an invitation he was happy to accept.

During my audit, I discovered that the partner not only charged for a full day at the golf event, amounting to £2500, but he also purchased an £80 pair of golf shoes, all of which was charged to the client.

I have seen numerous examples of this billing in my career at all sizes of firms and in various jurisdictions. In the last few years, I audited a trust company bill that charged a client for dropping flowers off at her mother's grave. When questioned about it, the excuse was: 'I log all my time, and it is for someone else, in accounts, to change it to non-chargeable time.

The 'Golf shoe case' was not pleasant as the lawyer, a notoriously aggressive lawyer, telephoned me to question who I was and why I was interfering with his relationship with his client. The case took months to settle as the firm was also very aggressive and unresponsive to the issues.

Dealing with legal costs and disputes between a client and a lawyer can be complicated. In my experience, the more aggressive the opposition, the more issues the law firms have concerns about. During the first telephone call with Mr Golf Shoe's lawyer, he aimed 'F bombs' at me like a market trader. He had something to hide!

In 2010, I had a client who was involved in a legal costs dispute with a major national law firm involving fees of approximately £80,000.

I attended their City of London offices, where I was met by the junior partner, who was slightly nervous introducing himself. He informed me, or should I say warned me, that a senior partner from 'up North' had travelled down that day for this meeting.

I was further warned that he was very unhappy with my client's attitude and non-payment of outstanding fees. After a few moments, in walked the senior partner, who was a wretched man, just as the junior partner had warned. He proceeded to let me know, in no uncertain terms, just how angry the firm was. After a few minutes of the deluge of F-bombs in his raised voice and overly aggressive behaviour, I decided enough was enough. I stopped him dead in his tracks. At that time, I had been in training for the veteran world karate championships in Portugal. I had spent the previous four months training very hard and dieting to get down my ideal fighting weight. It was the last week of training, and being so close to fight time, let's just say one becomes very tetchy.

The most critical lesson in law is preparation, preparation and then some more preparation before meetings with clients, court hearings and especially the opposition.

This law firm did not charge clients' travel time for fee earners moving between the various offices nationwide. What they did have, however, is a policy of charging for the fee earners travelling first class rail.

I raised this issue and asked if this was company policy. Strange how the mood changed, how the said aggressive partner left the meeting within 10 minutes and left me to negotiate with the 'good cop' partner. A deal was done, way below the £80,000.

How an average client deals with this type of unprofessional bully boy behaviour is beyond me.

I met the 'Golf shoe case' client on a boat to Portsmouth many years later as I was off to do another audit. I said, 'It would be interesting if I find a "golf shoe" issue on this case.'

He replied, 'Jim, you always do!'

What a sad indictment of the legal profession in the 21st century!

Chapter 6
Game Changer

My work with Goldman Sachs in 2003 happened because of a friendship I formed in 1985 playing, of all things, football.

As a Liverpudlian, football was a massive part of my teen years. At 16, I played in the Liverpool Sunday league, which, at the time, was the biggest in Europe with something like ten divisions. I played in the league's top division for a team called The Bedford, a multicultural team based in Toxteth. The Bedford had received some fame the year before I joined them. A former player, Howard Gayle, became the first black footballer to play for Liverpool FC.

The Bedford's home games were played in Sefton Park, and I remember when we had away games, we would meet at the Rialto, a prominent building on the corner of Parliament Street and Princess Park. Sadly, the Rialto was the first building to be burnt down during the 1981 riots.

In 1985 the law firm I worked for, Clifford Turner, had a football team which played in the London legal league. It was fun with matches being played under the floodlights of salubrious places like Hackney or Paddington Rec. Clifford Turner's trainee lawyers also got to play for the London trainee football team. In the spring of 1985, the group had been invited to participate in a competition at the same time as their annual conference in Liverpool.

In the mid-1980s, Liverpool still dealt with the aftermath of the riots and the city's economic downturn, so a weekend away was not high on people's agendas. How different it was these days (well, pre-Covid) with Liverpool now being one of the top venues for stag and hen parties.

The London Trainees were struggling to get an entire team, and someone suggested I should be invited because it was my town. First, to make up the numbers and second, to be the team's unofficial minder.

On the train to Liverpool, the organiser, who had researched where to go in Liverpool, announced that after the footy and legal conference, we would 'boogie the night away' at a local nightclub. He had found a couple of clubs to choose from, either 'The She' or 'The State'. Put it this way; I went to one of these clubs once, so the idea that about 12–14 public school-educated young men going clubbing at these venues in the 1980s still sends shivers down my spine.

I told the organiser that neither of these clubs was suitable for this illustrious group and suggested a club that would better suit them. He was happy to listen to my suggestion and would leave it up to me to organise the nightlife.

The weekend went fabulously. I got the guys into Tuxedo Junction, a top club and one where I knew the bouncers. The main bouncer I knew from my karate days at the Childwall Karate Club in Liverpool.

The one thing I'll give those public-school guys is that they know how to party. At one stage, all of them were on the dance floor surrounded by Liverpool girls who were smitten with their posh accents, crazy shapes and funky clothes.

I remember a guy approaching me semi-jokingly, asking what a bunch of 'southern w..kers' were doing on the dance floor. I remember sarcastically agreeing with him as they were being swooned over by the girls in the club, and he and his mates were propping up the bar. I bet those guys went off to dance lessons the following week and changed their names to Charles and Edmund.

My roommate for the weekend was the team's dynamite right back, Mr David Grounsell, a Clifford Turner trainee solicitor. Although we lost touch after that weekend, David got back in touch 18 years later, asking for my input on some legal costs issues in the company he was working for. He was the number two in-house lawyer for UK and Europe at Goldman Sachs International (GS).

David subsequently invited me to do an in-house seminar for the entire legal department at GS on external legal costs and how they could be controlled. Research I had previously carried out saw the US marketplace about 10 years ahead of the UK marketplace with in-house legal departments producing their own billing protocols for their external law firms to comply with. The American Lawyer magazine had in fact published a book on this subject, which included examples of such from the likes of Boeing and Morgan Stanley.

I drafted a six-page client retainer document for them to consider using for their external law firms. I believe the final version was submitted around the legal marketplace and caused such a stir that it was referred to in Legal Business Magazine 2003.

Sadly, although this was another possible game changer, it seemed to fizzle out. That was until I produced *"The Client Guide to Controlling Legal Costs"* a decade or so later. I am on working on 4th version, it will be available in Summer 2023 on my website www.jimdiamond. com for free.

Chapter 7
Legal Costs Budget Software Programme

I had no interest in IT or software but could see the advantage of budget software as a benefit for clients and law firms trying to comply with the professional conduct rules.

In 2001, I developed the budget software programme with my IT genius. The programme calculated legal fees from minor personal injury cases to commercial litigation disputes up to £5 million in value.

The software took over 18 months to develop and is ground breaking. The software's unique selling point (USP) was that it contained the data of the cases as a benchmark rather than having to produce a detailed budget from scratch.

During the following 12-month period, I demonstrated the software to small law firms, the biggest city of London law firm, and a raft of in-house legal departments.

I was invited to present the budget software at the 2003 annual Law Society of England and Wales conference at the Queen Elizabeth buildings in Westminster. I travelled to London the day before and stayed at the Crowne Plaza Hotel overlooking the River Thames and the Houses of Parliament. I can remember feeling apprehensive as I walked across Westminster Bridge to the venue on the morning of the conference. There were hundreds of people in attendance, and I had to present my legal budget software to what I correctly presumed to be a cynical audience.

I think the presentation went smoothly, but the response to the exhibition was muted, and the take-up of the software programme was zero.

In 2004, I was asked to provide a similar presentation to a group called Commerce and Industry (C&I), an offshoot of the Law Society dedicated to solicitors who generally work in-house in large companies' legal departments.

At that time, most in-house legal departments contained fewer than five lawyers. The presentation went far better than expected, and an arrangement was made in which the C&I group would fully endorse my software programme to their members, approximately 2000. The quid pro quo of this endorsement was that I would provide a telephone advisory service to all their members for 12 months free of charge, which I was happy to do.

My 12-month arrangement with the C&I group finished in early 2005. Not one of the 2000 members took a free version of the budget software for review.

One in-house lawyer discussed the possibility of rolling the programme out to his panel of lawyers, including one national law firm with whom I had previously done some legal cost consultancy work.

The lawyer presented his proposal to said law firm, but their response was a resounding no, so that project was scuppered before it started.

Also, in my initial presentation to the C&I committee, one of the concerns voiced was whether I would have the capacity to be able to provide the free telephone advisory service to all their members. I assured them I would.

In the 12 months over which the arrangement ran, I did not receive a single phone call from any of the 2000 members of the C&I on any aspect of commercial legal costs.

Towards the end of 2004, I gave a seminar on my budget software to the now retired Deputy Senior Cost Master, Mr John O'Hare, at the Royal Courts of Justice (RCJ), in London.

Master John O'Hare, whom I believed had faith in the software programme and the whole concept of legal budgets for the betterment of the legal system in the UK, pulled a few strings to get me an invite to the Judges and Costs Judges forum to present my software programme and my views on legal budgets.

The nervousness I had felt walking across Westminster Bridge to present at the Law Societies conference paled in comparison to the feeling I had on the morning of 5 May 2005, driving to central London to give a 45-minute legal budget seminar to the 50 delegates, 30 of whom were judges.

I can remember parking the car two hours before I was due to talk and walking along the embankment, collecting my thoughts. I have no idea what people must have thought walking past me, but I'm sure I was acting out the seminar and probably presenting it on the streets of London. The two hours flew past, and before I knew it, it was time for me to take the long walk up to the doors of the RCJ (see photo on the front cover of the book). It was daunting.

Even though it is truly a magnificent building, my only thought as I entered it was, I'm so looking forward to walking out of here in two hours.

While preparing for the seminar the previous day, I photocopied 100 screenshots of the PowerPoint presentation I had prepared. I had this nagging feeling that the RCJ's IT Department would lose or make a mess of what I had sent them. I walked into the building and put my documents on the scanner. A security guard questioned why I had so many papers. He didn't suspect me of anything; he was just curious as he rightly assumed that the documents must be heavy. The walk along the corridors was magnificent and breathtakingly scary to a participant in the gladiatorial litigation arena.

I was the first speaker after lunch, so most delegates were in their seats; I started my presentation. I walked up to the podium, put the papers on the floor and opened my laptop to connect to the PowerPoint loaded on the RCJ's server.

To my absolute horror, it would not connect. I can remember my breath getting deeper and deeper and my heart pounding faster and faster as I realised my PowerPoint presentation in front of the judiciary was not going to work. The conference organiser was frantically making calls to the IT department who were clearly on late lunch as nobody responded.

I started my presentation in front of the great sound of the Judiciary with the opening line of 'Looks like the PowerPoints f***** up'. Well, I thought about using that expression but what I said was, 'It looks like the PowerPoint is not working'. I am cynical about depending on other people, but in this instance, it paid dividends. I reached for my backup papers and distributed them among the delegates.

Forty-five minutes later, my presentation was complete, and the overall seminar finished an hour later. Without hesitation that in the 25 years, I have been giving workshops that was by far the best in content and reaction from those present.

During 2009–2013, the civil legal system was overhauled by reforms under the guidance of Lord Justice Jackson. He presented the first draft of the proposed rule changes in June 2009 at the Commercial Litigation Association (CLA) annual conference. Budgets and cost management were the main topics being reviewed for modification. I was also asked to speak at this conference and present my views on the subject. Lord Justice Jackson said first and discussed the draft rule changes from an academic perspective.

When it was my turn to present, I discussed the practical aspects of the subject. The first issue I raised with the top commercial lawyers in London was a request for a show of hands of those who'd produced a formal and detailed budget for their clients during their working life.

About five people raise their hands out of the nearly 100 delegates present. I believed from his expression that Lord Justice Jackson was surprised that so few field experts had practical experience formulating budgets.

In 2012 the Law Society approached me regarding producing a book on cost management for their members. In their view, with Lord Justice Jackson's reforms due to be introduced in the next 12–18 months, lawyers and law firms needed to develop skills in that area.

Over the next six months, after a lot of back and forth, it was finally agreed that I would produce a cost management toolkit including my budget software, various other budget templates, hourly rate surveys and various other documents and templates. The definitive version was fully endorsed and published in November 2012 by the Law Society, reasonably priced at £49.99 for everyone within the firm to use. This was a bargain as the usual practice with software is to sell it per user.

A word to the wise. Anyone who believes there is money to be made publishing anything with the Law Society, I have to curb your enthusiasm. A writer's fee is only 5–10% of the publication fee. So, don't plan to give up your day job.

In the summer of 2013, I was invited to be a panel member of the Law Society's Road trip to the local law societies throughout England and Wales. I accepted the offer, and the publicity material, including my toolkit on cost management, was sent out to all 150,000 Law Society members. This was a big commitment for me, but it was by far the best way of promoting work. Then, a day or so into the trip, I was abruptly removed from my primary role as a speaker.

A significant cost agency became one of the main sponsors of the road trip, and, to cut a long story short, I was relegated to a minor role as a substitute speaker. My participation would depend on other speakers dropping out or the number of local law societies that wanted the seminar. I cannot begin to explain just how disrespectful that behaviour by the Law Society was. It was also a massive slap regarding my work on the toolkit and my expertise in this field.

I was promised I would be involved in other conferences, road trips and seminars. However, a decade later, I am still waiting for those invites.

The irony of this is that I believe most of the conferences on the road trip were cancelled due to a lack of interest by the local law societies in England and Wales. I think one regional law society had only two potential delegates while there were four or five speakers.

The toolkit was removed from the Law Society's library five years after publication in 2018 due to being outdated. At that time, it sold less than 20 copies. Even when the price was reduced to half-price, it never generated any kind of response.

There are in 2021, just under 153,000 solicitors in England and Wales.

Chapter 8
Jersey – Legal Costs System

General

In 1999, the Jersey legal system on legal costs was fundamentally changed to align with the rules and regulations used in England and Wales. The Jersey costs rules mirrored almost exactly the 100 pages of the English regulations introduced in April 1986.

I say almost precisely, save one entire paragraph; a critical paragraph was deleted. The erstwhile section contained the rule which allowed a client the right to challenge their own law firms' legal costs.

In Jersey, clients wishing to dispute legal fees submitted by their lawyers can apply to the Jersey Law Society for the costs of mediation services they offer to the local marketplace.

It seems like a fair system, save for one fundamental problem. If a Jersey law firm does not consent to the mediation process, the Jersey Law Society has no power to order them to do so. In reality, the chances of mediation on a legal costs system in Jersey are slim.

The 1999 rule changes were meant to bring a new and fair way of judging litigation costs in Jersey. The fundamental problem of hi-jacking a system from another jurisdiction, a system that was in effect obsolete as a month before Jersey introduced their new rules, England and Wales introduced radical changes to their regulations on costs under Lord Woolf's reforms. In 2022, Jersey's rules on expenses are still fundamentally the same as rules used back in 1986 in England and Wales.

Having worked in the English and Wales system since its introduction in April 1986, I was asked to assist and comment on the best way to achieve their goals and identify potential practical issues. Let's just say I was livid when the authorities decided to remove the protection of the client in the rule-gathering exercise.

During this period, I gave in-house seminars to various Jersey Law firms and the Law Officers Department on the rule changes. At these seminars, I would regularly talk about the injustice of such a situation. I warned of the dangers, the potential explosion of legal costs and how access to justice would be explicitly affected for the low-income residents. The controversy hit the local press in June 1999. I have continued to question the system over the last 20 years.

In May 2021, the Jersey court could allow an hourly rate of £600 for a partner of a Jersey law firm against a litigant in person. On what was a simple procedural summons.

Optical Lens Case–Optical Services (Jersey) Limited v Carey Olsen [2018] JRC 140A

Petty Debts Court Greffier: (Mr D. Le Heuzé)

https://www.jerseylaw.je/judgments/unreported/Pages/[2018] JRC140A.aspx

The company's owner, Optical Lens Ltd, instructed me on a legal costs dispute involving them and a Jersey law firm, Carey Olsen (CO). After the main proceedings, the client was served a fully itemised bill of over £70,000. I was retained to audit the core papers and produce an itemised objection to the detailed bill of costs served by CO. I did this work for a fixed fee.

In layman's terms, the audit and production of the document are the comparisons of the work claimed in the bill of costs against counter figures of what I believe are reasonable or not.

I produced my detailed Points of Dispute, and the matter progressed to a paper assessment of the legal costs claimed by the greffier. I was contending that, in my professional opinion, the legal fees claimed by CO were excessive, unreasonable and disproportionate.

After a lengthy process, the Jersey Court produced a detailed report assessing the costs claimed and made the approached reductions, which included the following extracts from the judgment:

(ii) The reasonableness test will be based upon the English test as laid down in Francis v Francis and Dickerson [1953] 3 All E.R. at 836:

'When considering whether or not an item in a bill is "proper", – the correct viewpoint to be adopted by a Taxing Officer is that of a sensible solicitor sitting in his chair and considering what in the light of his then knowledge is reasonable in the interest of his lay client... the lay client... should be deemed a man of means adequate to bear the expense of the litigation out of his own pocket – and by "adequate" I mean neither "barely adequate" nor "super-abundant".'

(iii) Disbursements shall be allowed to the extent that they are actually and reasonably incurred and are reasonable in amount.

(iv) Research – it is expected that reasonably competent lawyers have sufficient expertise and are up to date in the law in the field in which they practise. In addition, research may also be considered as normal overheads as it will develop a fee earners knowledge in that area of law. However, a charge might be allowed for legal research on unusual, infrequent or unexpected points (Perry and Another v The Lord Chancellor, Times Law Reports, 26.5.1994). Where a claim for substantial research is made, I would expect evidence of that research on file. Fee earners would be expected to have at least a general knowledge of the additional point being researched and should record the reasons why the additional research is justified. A generalised attendance notes not backed by this evidence is unlikely to be successful. However, it is acknowledged that practitioners cannot be expected to be "walking law libraries" (Johnson v Valks. Court of Appeal 15 March 2000) and it may be reasonable to allow sufficient time for reviewing established law or procedural rules provided reasons are evidenced on the preparation notes.

(v) Fee Earners – it will be unusual that a fee earner will be able to claim for attendance (or other such communication) with other fee earners in the same organisation and working within the same

category of law. Evidence would need to be provided to justify why it was necessary for the fee earner with conduct of the case to seek advice from a colleague given that fee earners should be given cases that are within their competence. In addition, time spent on supervision of a fee earner should generally be viewed as part of the organisation's overheads.

(vi) Administration, e.g., photocopying, simple letters and emails forwarding documents or confirming receipt of documents or telephone calls checking availability or reminder of appointments already made, would be expected to be subsumed as part of the associated attendance or to be part of the lawyer's normal overhead expense being factored into the current Factor A rates.

(vii) I find it unreasonable to allow for items when there is no active work being carried out and will not allow items such as uncompleted telephone calls for when the person is not available or any care and conduct uplift for items such as travel and waiting time.

(viii) The letters and note of telephone calls on file will generally be sufficient to justify the unit charge for these items – normally one unit (a unit being six minutes) – please see section 3.0 'Specific Matters of Taxation' Practice Direction RC05/11. Ordinarily, the time entry would be sufficient for this evidence and I would not look behind the advocate's certification – see paragraph 28 of Pearce v Treasurer of the States. However, when files are called for taxation; I would expect to see the letters and/or emails to assess reasonableness using tests outlined within this letter – Practice Direction RC 09/01 paragraph 3.2.

(ix) For other preparation and attendance, including longer letters and telephone calls being claimed on a time basis, all time spent by the fee earner should be recorded on the file. In Brush v Bower Cotton and Bower [1993] All ER 741 (4), having considered Frascati, (Re: 2 December 1981, unreported), QBD and Johnson v Reed [1992] All ER 169, the court stated:

'Claims for unrecorded time are likely to be viewed with considerable care on taxation and it would be in an unusual case that any substantial allowance be made...'

Such time claimed will be allowed where it is clearly supported by the evidence from the file. This may include the length and complexity of the letters or other documents prepared or considered, the preparation notes and the handwritten notes of the attendance. Where no such record has been kept; consideration will be given to Rule 12/4 of the Royal Court Rules 2004 and my comments in paragraph 5.

It should be noted that, even where preparation has been fully recorded, the amount of time spent must be proportionate and reasonable.

The claim for legal costs was reduced to £9724.90. A massive 80% reduction.

The case is self-explanatory regarding legal costs. However, one further issue is relevant and, again, self-explanatory.

The initial judgment was made on 10 November 2016 and contained the following paragraph:

1.2 Mr Kenny has been assisted by Mr Diamond, who styles himself as a "Costs Lawyer". While I do not doubt Mr Diamond's expertise within the English legal field, I do not have any information regarding his qualification within the Jersey legal arena or other jurisdictions. I have tried researching Mr Diamond's website, which displays an impressive portfolio of published articles and long-term employment within respected legal firms, but unfortunately, his qualifications are not listed. I cannot, therefore, make any assessment of his expertise within the Jersey jurisdiction regarding legal costs. I have taken the view that Mr Kenny's reply should be treated as replying as Litigant in Person.

Few times in my 40+ year career have I been as incensed as when I read this extract, which belittles my expertise, experience and legal qualifications. The rest of the judgement did not mention fee earners who worked on the case at the law firm. It just commented on me!

The Grieffier had only reviewed a blog I wrote, not my actual website. He was also unaware of my work experience and the numerous articles I had published on the Jersey legal marketplace. One of the reasons the claim for costs was reduced by over 80% was the use of the case law in the audit report I produced, the majority of the legal authorities I referred to being English cases introduced the decade before Jersey adopted the English system.

So being Jersey qualified would have been of little advantage as these authorities would not be in their everyday working experience.

It took me two years to get the judgement regarding paragraph 7.2 amended to the following.

Mr Kenny has been assisted by Mr Diamond who is a practising Costs Lawyer registered with the UK Regulatory Costs Lawyer Standards Board. However, Mr Diamond is not a Jersey qualified solicitor or Advocate.

Hardly a sparkling endorsement of my work to produce the most significant percentage reduction of a law firm's claim for legal costs I have obtained in my 40-year career in any jurisdiction.

Note – I have never received any work/instructions to advise on legal costs following this judgement by any Jersey law firms, professional advisors or trust companies.

2012 – Jersey Moves into The Lord Justice Jackson! (Or Did It?)

In the winter of 2012, the former president of the Jersey Law Society requested a meeting with me to discuss the Jersey legal system and the changes forecast on the mainland with the imminent changes under the Lord Justice Jackson reforms.

We finished the meeting with the plan that I produce a report on my views of the possible changes in Lord Justice Jackson's reforms, costs budgeting and ideas as to how Jersey could synchronise with the modern world on legal costs.

We also discussed the organisation of the first-ever Jersey Law Society dedicated legal costs forum, where I would be one of the main speakers.

My report would be produced on the basis that it would be published on Jersey and Guernsey Law Reports website, which would be a superb marketing tool for my professional services.

I spent a considerable amount of time producing the report. To my dismay, the former editor of Jersey and Guernsey Law Society did not publish it, even though the former President of the Jersey Law Society thought it worthy of doing so.

Moving on to the Jersey Costs Conference, I did considerable prep work for my presentation and my introductions to several potential other speakers.

The week before the conference, I received an email from the former president of the Jersey Law Society saying he had received negative feedback about my Legal Costs Lawyer status.

I had to supply my Costs Lawyer practising certificate to the former president of the Jersey Law Society, who forwarded it to the specific dissenting person, the same former editor of Jersey and Guernsey Law Society.

The conference took place in February 2013 at The Radisson Hotel. Besides myself, some senior English lawyers were present and a QC and Deputy Judge.

Before my presentation, I was introduced as the man who had been more critical of the Jersey legal costs system over the previous decade than anyone else and was now here to bring Jersey into the modern costs management budget era.

I thought I had simply been professionally doing my job.

The former editor of Jersey and Guernsey Law Society did not attend. However, many Jersey lawyers, politicians, members of the press and lay people did.

Overall, at the end of the conference, there was a positive response from the delegates. Usually, as part of the document package, delegates at these conferences receive a feedback form with a comment section for them to fill in based on their experience of the course and the speakers. Generally, delegates complete these forms unsigned and include little or no negative comments, or if they do, they are often vague comments such as 'Didn't like the sandwiches and the like.

A week or so after the conference, the organiser sent me an unredacted version of the comments received for my presentation, one of which was:

"Engaging, Controversial, Bit of Barrow boy. But worth listening to."

Bit of a barrow boy! I'm a Liverpudlian coal man's son; my father would turn over in his grave at that comment.

Chapter 9
-JIMMY DIAMOND (Dad)

If your life is defined by a series of moments or events, my first occurred on 7 May 1980.

It started as just a typical day. I had been working in Liverpool city centre. I had trained after work and got home around 7 pm.

Mum had cooked – I think it was pie and chips, it was always something with chips. My mum and younger sister then went to bed, leaving my dad and me to watch the Wednesday night football on Granada TV.

I was in my late teens and could count on the fingers of one hand the times I had spent with my dad, just the two of us. With six children, his own business to run, and being a fanatical fisherman, I never seem to be a priority to him.

My dad was not a massive football fan but liked to watch the big games on TV. He must be one of the only Liverpudlians I have ever known to have never attended a live football game. As I was the star of my junior school football team, my dad came and watched me play once. In that game, our team won 3–2, and I scored three goals. I was not interested in the win or the goals but craved his attention. Sadly, he was just annoyed at me at the end of the game as I took too long to get changed.

The match that Wednesday night was a big one. It was the UEFA cup final between Eintracht Frankfurt and Borussia Mönchengladbach.

Towards the end of the first half, one of the prominent German defenders kicked the ball back towards the goalkeeper. However, it flew into the back of the net. It was a bit of a comical own goal, and I remember laughing and telling Dad this. I remember his rebuff very clearly, "Don't be bloody stupid! It wasn't"

They played the replay, and the commentator confirmed my view that it was an own goal. I looked at my dad, but he could not look at me as to do so would mean he would have to say he was wrong. My dad, in his world, was never wrong.

You could feel the tension in the room. It was a stupid own goal; it should never have mattered. Ten minutes later, my dad simply stood up, picked up his coffee cup walked into the kitchen to drop it in the sink. As he started to walk up the stairs, there was a muted 'night' from him. This was to be the last word he ever spoke to me.

I watched the end of the game on my own, relieved that the tension had gone. I switched the television off before midnight and went to bed. I suppose in those busy, active days; sleep was an easy friend.

Just after one is, my mum, incredibly stressed, came into my bedroom and woke me up. I still remember the red fluorescent light on my alarm clock flashing the number 1.16.

I remember trying to decipher Mum's words, but as the adrenaline kicked in, I knew something was seriously wrong. I went into her bedroom to see dad lying in bed, having a major heart attack. I remember Mum asking me to call the ambulance and to call my older brother. The following 30 minutes were just a haze. My older brother turned up, and we managed to get Mum to go downstairs. My brother attempted CPR. Suddenly there were no gasps of air, just silence. My brother went downstairs to tell Mum.

Over the years, I have been haunted by the sounds of my mum crying and sobbing after my brother told her. I stayed with Dad on my own for another 15 or 20 minutes until the ambulance arrived. I remember letting the two ambulance men in the house and showing them to the bedroom.

I remember them examining Dad briefly, but they knew he had gone. They put him on some type of stretcher and suggested that someone should go with them to the hospital. I grabbed hold of some clothes and followed the ambulance in the car.

An hour or so had passed since this craziness entered my life. The car journey, about three miles through the deserted streets of Liverpool to Broad Green Hospital, was surreal. Almost no cars were on the road, and the silence was a relief from the sobbing I had left behind.

I remember parking the car and walking into the deserted A and E department. A nurse came up to me and asked why I was there. I said my dad had just been brought in and thought he had had a heart attack. They took me into a small private room and sat me down.

They said nothing to me other than asking if I wanted a cup of tea. The cup of tea arrived with a saucer and what must have been half a packet of sugar. The adrenaline was now subsiding, and reality was kicking in. I'm not sure if it was 10 or 20 minutes or longer that I was listening to this sound of my teardrops splashing into my cup of tea. The nurse returned to the room and asked if I wanted to see Dad. I knew from her body language that he had died. The nurse took me to a small operating theatre. Dad was on the operating table, with a white sheet covering his body to his shoulders. I walked up and saw him and felt relieved for him that he was at peace after seeing him in such pain in the convulsion in his bedroom, which I had seen an hour or so before.

I have lived with tremendous guilt over the years that I could not comfort him or kiss him goodbye.

I sat in the car in the hospital car park for 20 minutes, trying to wake up from this bloody nightmare and dreading returning home. I don't know why, just an automatic reaction, but I put the radio on. The record playing was Bill Withers' "Ain't No Sunshine when you Gone". I have hated and loved that song equally over the years, but whenever I hear the first three bars, I remember every detail of that night.

In August 2012, I took my mum to the cemetery to drop flowers off at my sister's grave, and we talked about that night for the first time. She hadn't known until then that I had gone to the hospital and sat with Dad. When I told her, she said, 'That must have been so hard for you!' Those eight words released the guilt I had been carrying for over 30 years. The pain that never ends.

Dad, I have missed you so much over the years.

My Ma never fully recovered from that night and the loss of Dad and spent the next 38 years waiting to be back with him. I am happy for her that she now is.

I have never had a cup of tea with sugar in it since that night, and Eintracht Frankfurt went on to win the UEFA cup on away goals after the tie ended 3–3 on aggregate.

Chapter 10
The International Bar Association

In October 2011, I received an unsolicited email from Rebecca Lowe, a chief reporter at the International Bar Association (IBA).

Miss Lowe had seen my articles published in the legal press over the previous 12 months. The IBA found the subject very compelling, and they were considering doing a feature on legal costs.

We met at the IBA offices in the City of London. Miss Lowe asked me if I would mind being recorded. I wasn't particularly bothered either way, but I must admit I'd never had a meeting like this ever recorded. Maybe the IBA records everyone, but as I said, I wasn't bothered.

We decided that the best course of action would be for Miss Lowe to contact various experts from the field of legal costs and ask them to contribute to an independent and thoroughly researched article for publication in IBA's in-house magazine.

Other than contributing to the article, my crucial role would be providing Miss Lowe with information and guidance on the legal costs system.

Over the next six months, I gave Miss Lowe a wealth of information, including a list of people she could potentially interview for the article.

The IBA had their list of contacts, which included some of the major city law firms, whom they were able to approach for further input. The first phase of the project went well.

On 22 May 2012, Miss Lowe sent me an email which included the quote:

*"You're really not popular at city firms, are you?
I'm just beginning to get a whiff of it".*

I was fully aware of this view but was not concerned by it at all. Life is not a popularity contest.

I answered her other questions urgently as the publication day was 25 May 2012. On top of the considerable time I had spent over the earlier seven months, that added up and surprised me. I had not been expecting to spend the amount of time I did on the proposed article. Hopefully, it would be worth it as the IBA's in-house magazine had a worldwide membership circulation.

On 24 May, I received an email from Miss Lowe, which was possibly the most astonishing email that I have ever received in the whole of my 40-year career in the legal industry.

Hi Jim,

Sorry, my story has been spiked... you can probably guess the reasons why. The law firms hounded the IBA then the IBA dropped it. I am so sorry. It would have been a great piece, and I really appreciate your input. Hopefully, another time.

Best wishes, my apologies again.

Rebecca

From: Rebecca.Lowe@int-bar.org
To: jimdiamond@hotmail.co.uk
Subject: RE: jim
Date: Thu, 24 May 2012 09:30:11 +0000

Hi Jim,

So my story has been spiked... you can probably guess the reason why. The law firms hounded the IBA and the IBA dropped it. I'm so sorry. It would have been a great piece, and I really appreciate your input. Hopefully another time...

Best wishes, and my apologies again.
Rebecca

Rebecca Lowe
Senior Reporter

Work: +44 (0)20 7842 0096
Mobile: +44 (0)7702 786107
www.ibanet.org

International Bar Association
4th floor, 10 St Bride Street
London EC4A 4AD

Tel: +44 (0)20 7842 0090
Fax: +44 (0)20 7842 0091

the global voice of
the legal profession™ www.ibanet.org

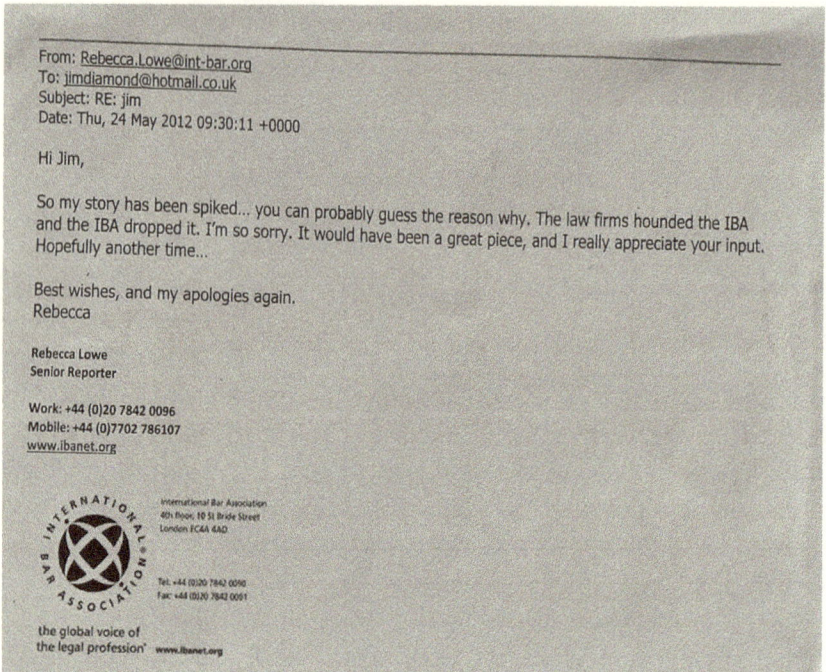

To say that I was furious would be a massive understatement. I tried contacting the IBA over the following months for details on whom and which law firms had hounded them, but my requests mostly fell on deaf ears. I say primarily because I received one e-mail from a member of the IBA board. In it, he stated that at no time had they been hounded by anyone, and they had just decided not to go ahead with the article.

I forwarded Miss Lowe's email dated 24 May to the IBA and awaited their response. There was none, and I never heard from Miss Lowe again.

The whole incident left a very bitter taste in my mouth. The extract below is taken from the IBA's website:

The foremost organisation for international legal practitioners, bar associations and law societies. Established in 1947, shortly after the creation of the United Nations, the IBA was born out of the conviction that an organisation made up of the world's bar associations could contribute to global stability and peace through the administration of justice. In the ensuing 75 years since its creation, the organisation has evolved, from an association comprised exclusively of bar associations and law societies, to one that incorporates individual international lawyers and entire law firms. The present membership includes more than 80,000 personal international lawyers from most of the world's leading law firms and some 190 bar associations and law societies spanning more than 170 countries.

LIFE IS NOT A POPULARITY CONTEST-

A previous email from IBA commenting on my popularity at certain city law firms.

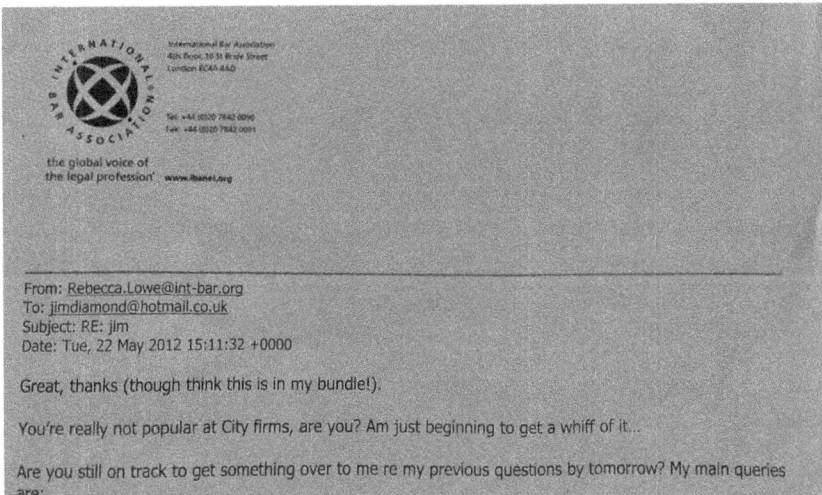

From: Rebecca.Lowe@int-bar.org
To: jimdiamond@hotmail.co.uk
Subject: RE: jim
Date: Tue, 22 May 2012 15:11:32 +0000

Great, thanks (though think this is in my bundle!).

You're really not popular at City firms, are you? Am just beginning to get a whiff of it...

Are you still on track to get something over to me re my previous questions by tomorrow? My main queries are:

Chapter 11
-2011- How Law Lost its Soul –
The epidemic of overcharging

In August 2011, I read an article in *Legal Week* about the profession of modern law firms. I contacted the editor and said I had a different viewpoint. We arranged to meet in a coffee bar in Wardour Street, London W1, where I gave him my draft article titled *How Law Lost its Soul – The Epidemic of Overcharging by City Law Firms*. Although somewhat taken aback, he did agree to publish it.

That article was probably the hardest-hitting and controversial of everything I have ever published. In the article, I looked at the turnover of the top 100 law firms, which had increased from £10.88 billion in 2005 to £13.7 billion in 2010. The 26% increase in turnover over those five years averaged over a 5% increase per year.

The 2019 turnover was £27 billion for the top 100 law firms. This is nearly a 100% increase since 2010, with an average increase of over 11% per year.

The article was published in September 2011; many months later I met the editor of Legal Week who thanked me for the article and informed me not one of the top city law firms had complained or even made comment on the article. The article is still online and over a decade later, not one comment from any top city law firms on it. Below is one of the comments made on the article.

Moment of Truth?

Thank you Jim Diamond - this is an excellent article - in fact one of the best I have read in Legal Week. The reason it is so good is because it dares to question City law firms' behaviour. There is nothing quite as refreshing as speaking truth to power.

The quote from a lawyer that 'one of the criteria (for gaining partnership) was whether I had the stomach and ability to 'milk' a case' - is a wonderful/tragic illustration of where we have got to.

But, perhaps Jim is only looking at the tip of the iceberg. Lawyers padding bills and making unreasonable charges is just the beginning. The real issue is the weakness of the General Counsel who pay the highly leveraged/inflation busting legal bills of external law firms without a thought - apparently without any concern for the financial harm this does to their company or the investments of shareholders.

Only one group of people can stop this, and that's the clients, but while corporate officers feel at liberty to spend 'other people's money' at will, little will change.

Also, because most shareholders in PLCs are in fact the general public - via the intermediaries of pension funds - City law firms are not just doing their clients a disservice they are ripping off the public at large. Which surely is a national issue and needs to be debated more widely? Perhaps a question in Parliament is needed?

Longtail -23 Sep 2011 | 10:52

Chapter 12
Clinical negligence

In 2016, the Centre for Policy Studies (CPS) commissioned a report on the ever-increasing legal costs of clinical negligence. The report's leading author was Professor Paul Goldsmith, and I was instructed to formulate a section on the personal injury market and market statistics (Goldsmith, 2016).

JIM DIAMOND SECTION ON NHS REPORT

INTRODUCTION

Diamond has worked in both sectors of the Personal Injury marketplace, including four years in-house for one of the biggest Defendant insurance law firms and running a Claimant Costs Company for three years; cases ranged from road traffic accidents to clinical negligence cases, costs disputes went from hundreds of pounds to seven figures. Overall, he has worked on approximately 1000 PI cases.

Introduction – The Costs War

https://www.judiciary.gov.uk/wp-content/uploads/JCO/Documents/Guidance/jackson-vol1-low.pdf

(The Costs War Page 27)

Although the 'Costs War' has been publicly raging for well over two decades between Claimant personal injury (PI) law firms and defendant insurance companies, the foundation of the 'Costs War' can be traced back even further to the mid-1970s.

In those days, the claimant PI law firms were the traditionally high street legal practices, offering a broad range of legal services with very few having more than ten partners. The defendant law firms were usually more prominent and dealt almost exclusively with insurance clients. The Claimant law firms saw themselves as 'freedom fighters' against the dominant and oppressive position of the corporate insurance world and the lack of legislation protecting the public.

Scale items of legal costs for successful litigants were still in force until 1986, when the brave new world of discretion for legal costs was introduced. It took a further 13 years for Lord Justice Woolf to establish his reforms to the civil legal system, especially his radical and what turned out to be disastrous changes to legal costs.

The advent of 'additional liabilities' following the introduction of 'No Win – No Fee' was primarily aimed at replacing legal aid for PI cases. The win fees and lawyers' win fees have cost the insurance world billions of pounds above the previous system.

The best example of the 'Costs War' following the introduction of Lord Justice Woolf's reforms concerned two cases. The first being Callery v Gray [2001] EWCA Civ 1117, which went all the way to the House of Lords on technical arguments, and the second was Hollins v Russell [2002] EWCA Civ 718; [2003] which allegedly involved 211,000 cases involving costs of over £1 billion.

This period also saw a growth in the claims management sector, the birth and death of the most significant two, Claims Direct and The Accident Group. The rocket ship went as down as quickly as it went up.

Although some of the reforms to the procedure on legal cases were a success in general, Lord Justice Woolf's reforms were a disaster for legal costs and specifically the PI industry.

Before Lord Justice Woolf's reforms, the hourly rates for PI lawyers were in the £100–£150 bracket for the claimant sector. The hourly rates for the Defendant sector were lower as the insurance industry had substantial buying powers to panel law firms.

Over the ten years following the introduction of the reforms, hourly rates increased. The bonus of introducing the 'No win – No fee' element gave the Claimant PI law firms a lift of up to 100% on rates. Straight forward road traffic cases saw law firms claiming up to £200 per hour (partner rates) as their introductory rates, with success fees added as high as 100%. So, gross rates of £400 per hour for straightforward PI claims were being claimed at the start of the 2000s.

The clinical negligence sector took this system to the extreme, with partners in central London law firms claiming basic hourly rates of £400–£450. With the addition of success fees of 100%, the gross rates being claimed exceeded £800.

The 'Costs War' has seen massive growth in the claims and sizes of law firms on both sides of the fence. The top law firms in both sectors are now multi-million-pound businesses. The rewards are enormous, so when Lord Justice Jackson was appointed in 2008 to review the civil costs system, both sides were entrenched in self-interest. The review took five years and backtracked Lord Justice Woolf's reforms by abolishing the additional liability concept.

Lord Justice Jackson's reforms were introduced in April 2013, but any cases signed up before this date, which there was an abundance of, will still be able to claim these additional liabilities for years to come. There is no specific data on the consequences of other disadvantages to the PI market as a whole, but there is little doubt that since the introduction in 1999 and the run of cases, the cost to the NHS service will be in the range of billions of pounds.

Clinic Negligence Cases (CNCs)

The simple message that comes out of doing research into CNCs is the staggering figures involved.

In its 2015–2016 annual report, the National Health Service's Litigation Authority (NHSLA) calculated that it would need up to

£56.4 billion to cover existing and anticipated liabilities (NHSLA, 2016). Although the body will pay out the damages over a period of decades, the figure is the equivalent to almost half the NHS's annual budget, which was £117.2 billion in 2015–16. The provision has increased this fiscal year significantly from £28.6 billion to £56.4 billion.

The most significant factor has been the change in the long-term discount rate set by HM Treasury from +2.2% to minus 0.8%. This change accounts for £25.5 billion of the total increase in the provision alone.

The NHSLA received 10,965 new clinical negligence claims in 2015–2016, compared with 11,497 received in 2014–2015. In the same period, they received 4172 new non-clinical liability claims, typically employers' and public liability claims, compared with 4806 in 2014–2015. The number of new clinical negligence claims fell by 4.6% last year, and the number of new non-clinical shares decreased by 13.2%. Nevertheless, 15,137 shares are substantial and represent a challenge for the NHSLA. In 2008/09, that figure was just 2373.

The defendant's market sector

It is far easier to criticise the claimant market sector. The sensational comments of 'ambulance chasers' and 'greedy lawyers' are continually screamed out from the public and press alike.

Well, let us look at the facts. Over the last three decades, the contentious work in clinical negligence has been outsourced to the Defendant insurance sector. This sector has consolidated into fewer than 15 leading law firms. These law firms undergo a panel process to get on and stay on the list as contracted suppliers.

The start of the 2000s saw some of these firms offering fixed hourly rates no matter the fee level for the earner who dealt with the work. The commercial sector attempted this 'blended rate' approach at the start of the 1990s, which ultimately proved unworkable.

The tendency was to keep lower grade fee earners on cases when at times, higher grade fee earners would have been more efficient.

A partner may charge a junior lawyer three or four times the rate, but his wisdom far outweighs the simple economics. Of relevance is that these major law firms are now substantial legal practices with revenue running into the multi-millions of pounds.

Little has changed in defending litigation over the last two decades. Lord Justice Jackson's approach to costs management was well versed in his draft paper on his proposed civil reforms produced in June 2009. There seemed to have been little appetite to embrace these reforms and develop them into an efficient way of defending clinical negligence cases.

I met the chief executive officer (CEO) of the Medical Defence Union (MDU) in or about 2011 at a Civil Justice Council forum. I explained to him that, in my opinion, it could be hugely beneficial to streamline the process to have a budget on the likely costs of all costs defending a clinical negligence case as early as possible with the aim of saving legal costs.

I was invited to present my Legal Costs Budget software package to the MDU. This quick and efficient program aims to produce simple cost budgets for various stages of a case. The software had a specific personal injury calculator. Attending the MDU offices one sunny May afternoon, I was somewhat taken aback to be met by only one member of the MDU, who took me to a coffee bar around the corner from their office for me to do the presentation. Not surprisingly, nothing progressed on this project with the MDU despite many reminders being sent over the next 12 months.

For the record, the MDU was offered budget software for free.

Lord Justice Jackson's reforms were introduced in April 2013, introducing costs budgets on most matters that progressed to the Case Management Conference ("CMC"). How an issue is dealt with indeed involves a quick assessment of the potential costs. The Law Society of England and Wales asked me in 2013 to produce a Tool

Kit on Costs Management in which I included the budget above software. This tool kit, in 2017, is still available in the Law Society publications.

In 2017, there were changes afoot, with the *Law Society Gazette* (Hyde, 2017) reporting:

The NHS Litigation Authority is to get a new name (NHS Resolution) and a new mission – to settle negligence cases early rather than fight them. Jeremy Hunt in the House of Commons said: "I can inform the house that the NHS Litigation Authority will radically change its focus from simply defending NHS litigation claims to the early settlement of cases, learning from what goes wrong and preventing errors."

At the end of 2016, the NHSLA developed mediation schemes following what they describe d as a successful pilot scheme (Hyde, 2016):

Valid. Two-year contracts were awarded to the Centre for Effective Dispute Resolution, Trust Mediation and Costs Alternative Dispute Resolution. The NHSLA did not reveal the value of these contracts but said it had secured "the highest quality mediation services for the NHS at the lowest possible cost".

The outcome of this scheme would undoubtedly shape clinical negligence cases in the future.

Claimant sector

Why not 'kill off the Claimant sector as they are all 'ambulance chasers' and 'money grabbing lawyers?

This theory has one fundamental flaw: who will represent anyone with a legitimate claim? While the PI war has raged for up to two decades, the public still needs an honest, cost-effective, efficient legal service to protect their rights.

An individual without this, even in the world of 'Google lawyers', will, in most cases, have very little chance of being successful and even less chance of achieving an appropriate damages package without proper legal assistance.

In terms of the problems in this sector, we have already discussed the issues created by Lord Justice Woolf's reforms which are now being reversed by Lord Justice Jackson's reforms. However, these reforms are still not dealt with other fundamental problems.

In 1991, in the High Court insolvency case, RE a Company (No 00408010f 1989 (1995) 2 ALL ER 155, the City of London Lawyers Association produced a set of statistics to show that the hourly court rates allowed winning law firms and payable by the losing side was wholly inaccurate and was damaging the legal system. In ballpark figures, the court permitted an introductory rate for central London law firms of between £80–£100 per hour, equating to about one-third of the actual hourly rates charged to clients by the majority of top London law firms.

Following the success of the RE a Company (No 00408010f 1989 (1995) 2 ALL ER 155 case, the basic rates claimed by winning law firms in central London exceeded £171 per hour. So started the law firms' calculations by law societies around the country to show the court rate was out of kilter in the commercial world of running a legal practice. However, high street law firms working in the civil legal aid system for clients were doing the same work at varying hourly rates depending on the classification of the work. If memory serves me correctly, at the start of the 1990s, basic preparation work was charged below £40 per hour, and items such as travelling and waiting were charged at less than £30. Move on a decade or so, and the courts started to produce guideline hourly rates for law firms around the country based on their location.

The current guideline hourly rates can be seen at: https://www.gov. uk/guidance/solicitors-guideline-hourly-rates. The highest rate is £409 per hour for a solicitor and legal executive with over eight years of experience in central London, and the lowest is £111 per hour for trainees, paralegals, or other fee earners in any location in England and Wales. However, these guideline rates do not differentiate between complex commercial or run-of-the-mill PI cases.

Here lies the first of the fundamental problems. A large percentage of PI work included in clinical negligence cases involves processing documents and administrative work, none of which should be charged near these hourly rates.

This issue regarding Woolf reforms was discussed in an article on hourly rates from *The Lawyer* in September 2010 (Byrne, 2010), which stated:

The most staggering figure within Jim Diamond's 2010 hourly rates survey was highlighted earlier this year by Lord Justice Jackson's review of civil litigation costs.

This revealed that some London-based clinical negligence lawyers earned as much as £900 an hour for advice.

Compare that with the hourly rate paid to junior doctors, who work up to 60 hours weekly for less than £20 an hour.

Claimant clinical negligence lawyers argue that the figure includes a success fee only when cases are won under the conditional fee arrangement regime.

Under proposals put forward by Jackson LJ, the recoverability of the success fee would be abolished, and the hourly rate cut dramatically. But Claimant lawyers warn this could have the unintended effect of blocking access to justice because lawyers would be choosier about the cases they take.

"We just wouldn't be able to afford it," one litigator claims. "The success fee pays for cases we lose."

But Jackson LJ has rejected such a notion.

"No evidence has been produced during the costs review to demonstrate that success fees at the levels currently charged are necessary to cover the cost of 'lost' cases," he has stated.

The Government and changes are currently considering the review are likely to be made to the system Lord Woolf introduced in 1999 – but it will not happen without a fight.

The days of the £900 hourly fee look to be numbered.

The second fundamental issue is the number of costs compared to the claim on a proportionality basis. This issue has been debated in cases reaching the Court of Appeal and has still not been resolved effectively.

The third and final issue relates to the time spent, and fees claimed compared to the costs agreed upon or assessed by the court. Like it or not, the claimant law firms consistently claim far higher prices than they are entitled to recover under the rules and regulations. However, very few actions can be taken by the Defendant's insurance companies, or the court can sanction this ridiculous situation. Legal costs become a market trade with winners claiming high and losers offering shallow figures.

For example, in simple terms, a claimant's costs are claimed at £100; the defendant offers £65, with a deal subsequently done at £75. In this example, unscrupulous Claimants or cost agencies, knowing the defendant simply wants a large percentage of the claim, may claim £150.

The court system

One cannot look at the problem without referring to the present court system. In February 2016, the Guardian reported that 86 courts in England and Wales were to be closed over 18 months (Bowcott, 2016).

This is quite astonishing, especially with the massive increase, as much as 600%, in court fees the year before. To issue a claim for £200,000, the court issue fee alone is £10,000. Should this increase not have had the opposite effect, in that the proposed extra revenue should enable other courts to be opened? This is not the case, and the system is instead grinding to a halt, with one set of courts in the South East of England announcing in 2015 that they had such backlogs that correspondence would now take ten weeks to be replied to (Law Society, 2015). This is a disgrace and an embarrassment to the legal system.

Conclusion

In a decade or two, we will be walking past old derelict hospitals that we can proudly tell our children are the mausoleum of what was the NHS – one of the most outstanding achievements of modern social society. Every one of us used a free service directly or indirectly, and we were humbled by the sheer professionalism, hard work and dedication of the majority who work within it.

And when our children ask us why our generation has let them down, we can refer them to one of the leading causes being the claims culture and 'Cost Wars'. We can tell them that a few 'killed it for the vast majority. We can say that some lawyers were highly greedy, while others on both sides of the fence let it ride as they feared change for self-interest.

UPDATE 2022

https://publications.parliament.uk/pa/cm5802/cmselect/cmhealth/740/report.html

42. The Government's evidence highlighted the extent to which costs have grown. They reported that claims against NHS providers had "increased four-fold between 2006–07 and 2019–20 from £0.6 billion to £2.3 billion" and the Government's total liabilities for clinical negligence "increased from £9 billion at 31 March 2007" to **£82.4 billion** by March 2021.[43] Furthermore, the Government's projections show that liabilities within the Clinical Negligence Scheme for Trusts (CNST) - the largest scheme which meets the costs of clinical negligence for NHS Trusts and accounts for 95 per cent of cash payments - could by the end of the decade snowball to **£155 billion** and annual cash payments could reach £4.3 billion

46. Claimant legal costs now account for 77 per cent of all legal costs within clinical negligence.[54] The Government's written evidence noted that since the mid-2000s the "average claimant legal costs per claim grew from **double to quadruple** the size of average defendant legal costs per claim."[55]

Chapter 13
-Photography

One piece of advice I would give anyone considering a lifetime in the law is to get another interest, one that doesn't involve the law, people in the law or one in which you can escape into a different world.

I can't remember how or why photography became a passion of mine. I remember getting a Polaroid camera as a kid, but I can't remember taking any pictures. However, somewhere along the line, after a long-term ankle injury in my early/mid-20s, I realised that competitive sport would end soon and wondered what I would do with the vast amount of spare time I would now have.

I suppose impulsion has always been in my nature. One lunchtime, while working at Clifford Turner, I walked into a Dixons store in Fleet Street and said to the salesperson, 'I need a camera. One that's good at taking sports photos.

Fifteen minutes later, I walked out of the store with a slightly above entry-level Nikon camera with a fixed 50mm lens. I think I went back to Liverpool that weekend and took some photos of the old dockland and cityscape from the top of the Anglican Church, the docklands and the deprived and falling areas of parts of Liverpool. I waited seven days to get the negatives processed and printed, and that's how the love affair started.

I returned to London and started taking photos of the karate fighters I was training with.

I realised early on that in photography, you get what you pay for, so the £400 entry-level investment camera needed to be upgraded.

The upgrade was a massive jump in quality, and so was the price. The two or three leading photography magazines at the time guided me to a Nikon F3. It was something like £2000–3000 for the body of the camera only and no lens.

There was no way I could afford those sums, so I went to the ad section in the photo magazine and discovered an almost brand new F3 being sold by a man in south London.

Arriving at his house some days later, I was a bit concerned as I had about £1000 in cash in my pocket, this time without the support of my family's heirlooms.

He was not the sort of guy you would buy a second-hand car from. He did know his photography stuff and suggested I also purchase a super-fast lens suitable for action sports photography, especially in areas with low light levels.

The deal was done, and I returned to my flat and took out the kit and instructions manual. That evening I discovered a leaflet at the bottom of the camera box with German writing and a particular reference to the British Army. Luckily my south London guy was legit, or I may have suspected the equipment was not 100% kosher.

In photography, like law, I was almost all self-taught. But when I have a passion for something, I go into intense detail during my learning process.

I am sure today there is some name or acronym used for it, but I suppose in my day, my personality could simply be described as being a 'pain in the arse' with obsession-like qualities such as not letting go of something until the end.

Over the next two years, I concentrated on taking photos of karate competitions in England, although I also travelled as far as France to the world karate championships in Paris.

I also worked as an in-house photographer for Mike Barratt, one of the top three boxing promoters in the UK. Although there was no money in it, it did provide the experience of covering boxing shows at venues such as The Royal Albert Hall. As I was working freelance in my legal day job at the time, I could manage the massive amount of time it needed.

These were great and simple times, but it was not sustainable as I simply could not make any money. Before camera phones and the like, I would constantly be asked to do 'social' type photography, such as weddings, christenings and birthday parties.

If you only do a few of these, it's ok, but when you do more than 20 or 30, it becomes dull, and I began to devalue what I wanted to achieve.

The love for photography disappeared almost as quickly as it had been found, and I had my 'sliding door moment' where I realised, I had to either continue and move full-time into photography or move back in-house with a city of London law firm.

At the start of 1990, I was offered a number two position at a top City of London law firm Allen & Overy, dealing with their contentious legal costs disputes.

By the end of January 1990, I had sold all of my camera equipment, which was the end of that story. That is until, as in so many parts of my life, a curve ball arrived in the form of a letter from Tiffany Stamp, the art coordinator at Vogue. I had sent examples of workaround to numerous publications over the previous five years, and I couldn't remember what I sent to Vogue. Their letter invited me into their offices to show them my work.

I had one or two sleepless nights but decided my mind had been made up, and I declined their kind offer to visit them and present my work.

I don't regret my decision; I don't regret continuing my photography career. I just knew I could not do both. The following five years saw me gain giant "big ticket" legal costs experience at Allen & Overy. On a personal front, I got married in 1991 and had four children in the decade.

In November 2019, I attended a white-collar boxing event at the Crown Plaza in Glasgow. I was a guest of a former boxer whom I once took promotional photographs of in the 80s. My passion was ignited that night, and I got back into photography with the same love I had in the 80s. In the last year, I have covered two world title fights. A number of small hall shows from York Hall in London to the Beach Ballroom in Aberdeen. If anyone is interested my portfolio is on IG jimdiamondphotography.

Chapter 14
Association of Costs Lawyers

A Costs Lawyer is a qualified and regulated legal professional who specialises in the law and practice of legal costs. Anyone wishing to qualify as a Costs Lawyer must undertake a three-year training course (equivalent to a degree-level qualification) and have three years of supervised costs practice before being recognised as a Costs Lawyer. Costs Lawyers are regulated by the Costs Lawyer Standards Board (CLSB). The CLSB is overseen by the Legal Services Board (LSB). All Costs Lawyers must also carry professional indemnity insurance.

There are three specific types of Cost Lawyers. The first type is those working in-house, which means they are working full-time in a particular law firm that will, more often than not, be one of the large commercial practices that can afford to have that service full-time. The second type is those working for independent legal cost agencies around the country. Some companies that work in that way are significant regarding numbers and turnover. The third and final type primarily works for a small number of law firms that use their service on an ad hoc basis. This type of lawyer is sometimes referred to as a kitchen table provider because they are independent and work at home at the kitchen or dining table, which is ironic as in these times of COVID-19, many of us now work from the kitchen table.

Within the industry, Cost Lawyers face a lack of recognition since they are not as high profile as solicitors or barristers. The Association of Costs Lawyers (ACL), which was formed in 1977 as the Association of Law Costs Draftsmen (ALCD), to try to address the situation by helping to promote the status and interests of the profession of law costs drafters while ensuring the continued maintenance of the highest professional standards. The association, which changed its name in 2011 following the recognition of Costs Lawyers in the Legal Services Act 2007, has an educational arm (ACL Training) and is the only place you can get the qualifications to be a cost lawyer.

I joined the CLA at the start of the 1990s when they had fewer than 200 members. Due to the increase in litigation over the next 30 years, there was massive growth in the industry. The Cost Lawyers' expertise is predominantly in personal injury, legal aid, matrimonial law and the criminal legal marketplace.

It is a very specialised part of the law. Yet, most people in this field are not ACL members, meaning they have no recognised qualifications and have probably received their training internally working for extensive legal practice.

There are many stories of non-ACL members being exposed for their work or advocacy at court because they lack the knowledge or work experience.

In 1998, I was invited to speak at a significant cost conference promoted by International Business Conferences (IBC) for approximately 80 delegates.

Apart from myself, the other panel members included industry stalwarts Michael Cook, the doyen of the legal cost world at that time, and Tony Girling, the ex-president of the Law Society.

To begin my presentation entitled 'The loaf of bread principle', I produced a loaf of bread and explained that clients might want this cheap white loaf or other more exotic forms of bread and although they are prepared to pay for different levels and standards of these products, they want quality at a price they can afford. In other words, stop making the process of costs law complicated. Work out the costs initially so a client can have the right price— hardly rocket science.

I then moved on to the question and answer (Q & A) section. I had prepared a budget for a semi-fictitious case and requested that the delegates produce ballpark figures for the costs of certain aspects of that particular case. One example was the likely cost of a barrister attending a six-month trial offshore on a multi-million-pound claim, i.e., the brief fee.

This exercise was intended to show the delegates and my fellow panel members the difference between legal cost disputes in which there are various rules and regulations as opposed to the prices of legal services, such as in the example given above.

The subtle differences between the prices depend on what the client (the sophisticated buyer of legal services) is prepared to pay. The court has no power over this agreement. In the same way, a court will have no control over the price you pay for your plumber to do a specific job at a fixed fee.

There was only a limited amount of information in the Q & A, but it was enough for me to show delegates and panel members that supply and demand will always be the foundations of the price of legal services.

Once the delegates had completed the exercise, I asked them to let me know by a show of hands who believed the barrister's brief fee would be under £200,000. Only two of the delegates said it would be more. When I revealed the actual brief fee on a case with familiar details was £400,000, the delegates and panel members were collectively 'surprised'.

Getting back onto the CLA, in 2010, *The Lawyer* magazine once again published my article on the hourly rates of the top city law firms. This article received tremendous publicity in the legal, national, and international press, showing that city law firms' rates had bounced back to pre-2007–2008 levels.

About six months after the publication of the 2010 survey, I received a circular email from a PR company stating they had been approached by the committee of the CLA about producing a definitive hourly rate survey. They further said they would be able to obtain unprecedented stats on hourly rates due to the size and diversity of the members of the Association.

My reply to this e-mail was short and succinct, 'there is more chance of me winning the Grand National on a rocking horse than there is of you producing a definitive hourly rate survey'.

Two weeks later and low-and-behold, an email was circulated to all the members of the CLA to inform them that the definitive hourly rate survey was going to be produced in conjunction with *The Lawyer* magazine. A questionnaire was sent from the PR company, which asked that members send them hourly rates from the marketplace they were currently working in. Knowing that some people might be reluctant to part with sensitive information, an incentive was offered where any member who followed the request and submitted the information would be put into a draw where the lucky winner would receive an iPod.

Yes, that's right, an Apple iPod!

As you can imagine, the collective response from the in-house cost lawyers was incredulity. The CLA asked members to send confidential information about their clients/employers for them to publish in The Lawyer magazine, all for the chance to win an Apple iPod.

I do believe that if any in-house Costs Lawyer would have been foolish enough actually to furnish the CLA with the confidential information, it would almost certainly have resulted in a breach of the employment contract and, I imagine, an on-the-spot sacking, but hey, they could always listen to their new iPod as they cleared out their desk and were escorted from the building.

I remember exchanging an e-mail with the editor of The Lawyer magazine stating the CLA would produce nothing but could damage my ten-year relationship with them. Her view was that it would be best if they tried to work with the CLA and see what they produce.

The CLA produced NOTHING. Save it did damage my relationship with The Lawyer.

I raised this issue with various committee members of the CLA over the years and had no response. In the early 00s, they even refused to publish/comment on my hourly rates survey in their internal magazine. The reason they gave was that the statistics were not relevant to the membership.

In my four decades of membership, the CLA has never invited me to be a speaker at any of their regional or annual conference.

Chapter 15
Legal Costs System in Scotland

In May 2018, I received a phone call from the client about a possible costs audit in Scotland.

I had been working in Scotland on another significant matter, so I had the work experience, but more importantly, I was also seen as someone who would 'fight' the Scottish legal system. The disputed fees exceeded £6 million; approximately £4 million for the law firm Levy & McRae and about £2 million for the junior advocate, Jonathan Brown.

Little did I know I would end up spending three years on this case, working through approximately 200 boxes of legal papers and ending up at loggerheads with the Law Society of Scotland (LSS) and the Faculty of Advocates (FOA).

So, I will keep the issues involved to just one succinct chapter. I can say that this was the worst case of overbilling a client I have come across in my 40+ years in the legal profession.

The actions and lack of efforts by the LSS and FOA deeply concerned me, not just regarding this case but regarding the overall protection of the general public in Scotland.

I initially contacted the FOA in May 2018 to request basic information on costs and regulatory disputes. Mr Brown's fees were more than £2 million. To my surprise, I received a detailed answer (18th May 2018, see below) from the then Treasurer of the FOA, Roddy Dunlop QC. The note expressed a thorough knowledge of the underlining case and costs dispute.

I did not know at the time that Roddy Dunlop QC was a member of the Axion chambers, the same chambers Mr Brown was a member of. I also was unaware that Roddy Dunlop QC was the lead counsel in the underlining case; in other words, Mr Brown was on the opposition side.

I received a direct call about 20th May 2018 from the then Dean of Faculty, Gordon Jackson QC, who said he would overview the case. He asked me to correspond directly with him and keep him up to speed. He also said that he thought the legal fees were 'eye-watering'.

Over the next month, there was little movement on the matter, but I felt there were issues in how the FOA was dealing with the case. I, therefore, issued a data notice request to them. To my astonishment, I discovered Roddy Dunlop QC had circulated his email exchange with me to various members of the FOA committee and, over the following two weeks, had also had email exchanges with Mr Brown.

I also discovered that the private and confidential correspondence between myself and Gordon Jackson QC had been circulated to committee members.

In April 2022, *The Herald* newspaper published an article regarding an example of professional misconduct by Gordon Jackson QC (Gordon, 2022).

A lawyer who successfully defended Alex Salmond during his sexual assault trial has been found guilty of professional misconduct for discussing the case on a train. Gordon Jackson QC, a former Labour MSP, was caught on video naming two women who had complained about the former First Minister.

While auditing the working papers, I found an email from Jonathan Brown referring to a 'liquid lunch' with Roddy Dunlop QC on the underlying cause. Although I am not for one second suggesting any impropriety was going on or has gone on, I am questioning how the public perceives this.

Over the next four to five months, I audited the entire collection of working papers. My view was and still is that this was the worst case of overcharging I have come across.

Litigation was issued regarding one specific legal point, and I was in charge of the audit and issuing regulator disputes against Levy & McRae and Mr Brown. Scotland has a two-tier complaints system which is used after sending an initial complaint with the law firm/ partner and advocate.

Stage 1

The 23 formal complaints against Mr Brown and the conducting partner, Graham Craik, at Levy & McRae, were submitted to the Scottish Legal Complaints Commission (SLCC). It took the SLCC approximately ten months to investigate these complaints, but they finally issued two formal eligibility reports against both. The SLCC deemed that 21 of the 23 complaints needed to be explored through stage 2.

Stage 2

Seven out of eight complaints against Mr Brown were referred to the FOA for them to investigate. Fourteen out of 15 complaints against Mr Craik were referred to the LSS.

This process took another two years, with the Complaints Committee of the FOA finding against Mr Brown on specific issues. A subsequent appeal by Mr Brown was dismissed.

The article below was published by *Scottish Legal* on their website on 19 January 2022 (Skilling, 2022).

An advocate whom the Scottish Legal Complaints Committee fined after it found he had failed to act in a client's best interests by failing to disclose the terms of a feeing arrangement to senior counsel before settlement negotiations have lost an appeal against part of the decision.

Jonathan Brown had been instructed to act for a Cayman Islands company, A and E Investments, in high-value litigation in the Court of Session. The Committee found that, in not informing lead counsel of a "success fee" payable to him by the company's controller, Robert Kidd, he had not acted in his best interests and his behaviour amounted to unsatisfactory professional conduct.

The Faculty of Advocates Disciplinary Tribunal considered the appeal. The tribunal noted that the legal validity of such success fees was the subject of ongoing litigation at the time the decision was made. For the purposes of the appeal, it was assumed that such a fee would have been payable.

Conflict of interest

Under the terms of the negotiated success fee, Mr Kidd was required to pay the appellant a fixed percentage of any sum awarded to A and E in excess of £10 million. This was calculated at 1% for every £100,000 received above £10 million, discounting any sum awarded as expenses. Following Mr Brown's instruction, senior counsel was also instructed to act for A and E; however, the appellant was instructed by the instructed solicitors not to inform him about the existence of the success fee.

Immediately before proof, the parties to the case entered settlement negotiations, with senior counsel taking the lead for A and E. It was argued by the appellant that it was not his responsibility to inform senior counsel of the success fee and that his unawareness would not have had a deleterious effect on Mr Kidd's interests during negotiations. However, the Committee took the view that the different feeing arrangements had the potential to cause a conflict of interest if an offer to settle was made.

It was further held by the Committee that the appellant should have noted that there was a possible conflict of interest between the instructing solicitors and Mr Kidd if, as was likely, their success fee was calculated in a manner similar to his own. The appellant did not, however, ensure that the conflict was removed or inform the client about the conflict.

The appellant contended that the findings of the Committee did not establish the complaint, as it did not find that he was obliged to tell senior counsel about the feeing arrangement. He had not done so based on a perception that it was in the client's best interests to preserve harmony within his legal team. It was also argued that a finding of unsatisfactory professional conduct was unreasonable and inappropriate in the circumstances.

Proper and informed manner

In its decision, the tribunal observed: "The Committee held that for counsel to act in a situation of conflict of interest between his own financial interests and those of his client amounts to conduct that would fall below the standard reasonably to be expected of a reputable and competent member of the Bar. That, it seems to us, is clearly correct. Although not technically in a fiduciary relationship with the client, counsel is at all times expected to act in a similar manner to those who are subject to formal fiduciary relationships."

It continued: "If evidence is led relating to a complaint that discloses unsatisfactory professional conduct (or professional misconduct), we consider that the disciplinary body is entitled to take account of such evidence and conclude that there is unsatisfactory professional conduct, or professional misconduct, provided that the evidence can be described as reasonably related to the complaint."

Addressing the appellant's arguments on appropriateness, the tribunal said: "We consider that it was essential that senior counsel should have a knowledge of the success fee arrangement to conduct the negotiations regarding settlement in a proper and informed manner. The success fees of both the solicitors and the appellant would form a major deduction from the principal sum received by the pursuers, and the amount of those fees would depend on the manner in which the settlement was structured. Senior counsel was obviously in charge of the settlement negotiations."

It continued: "His lack of knowledge of the success fee arrangements meant that he conducted those negotiations without knowing of an important consideration in the calculation of the ultimate sum that would be paid to his client. That in our opinion is a clear disadvantage; the client's primary interest is in the amount that he actually receives for his own benefit. It is equally clear that it was therefore essential that the existence of the success fee arrangement should have been disclosed to senior counsel."

On the relevance of the solicitors' instructions not to tell senior counsel about the arrangement, it added: "We do not think that that instruction is material for present purposes. Counsel is always expected to behave in a manner that is both independent and objectively justified. If necessary, an advocate can obtain independent advice. This is typically obtained from a Faculty Officer. In our opinion, standing the instruction not to inform senior counsel of the success fee arrangement, the obvious, and indeed the only, satisfactory course would be to take advice from a Faculty Officer."

The tribunal therefore rejected the appeal, concluding: "The need to avoid conflicts of interest, and in particular financial conflicts of interest, is of significant importance professionally, and we therefore consider that in a case where such a conflict has been allowed to emerge, without taking obvious remedial measures, a substantial penalty must be imposed. In all the circumstances we see no reason to interfere with the decision of the Complaints Committee."

Mr Brown received the maximum fine of £3000 and the Complaints Committee ordered a formal letter of reprimand be served on him. This decision was never appealed. The Deputy of FOA refused my request to have a copy of this letter of reprimand. An extraordinary decision in my view.

Further background issues regarding Complaints against Mr Brown.

Issue No 1

On 17th January 2020, Mr Brown's lawyers, Brodies, lodged a formal response to the complaints. On pages 9/10, para's 1.32 and 1.36

"We are concerned about the extent to which the SLCC may have placed on reliance on Mr Diamond's views".

"It is impossible for someone in his position to offer any meaning full view on the level of the fees without understanding the nature and extent of the instructions, the detail of what was done and why it was done".

The first issue is something with respect the SLCC should look into. I dealt with them during the complaints process, produced a detailed report, and that was that.

The second issue, again, is what I do. I audited over 100 boxes of papers over numerous months before submitting my audit report. I have defended and opposed some of the top QC's fees over the last 30 years in negotiation and on full costs hearings. Not least the fees of Jonathan Sumption QC, as was, and to later become Lord Sumption, head of the Supreme Court and often described as Britain's cleverest man. The case involved Nissan Japan and Octva Botner; the claim was in or above £600m. Perhaps re-read para 1.36 again to consider the credibility of this submission.

I was informed by a partner at Levy & McCrae that Scotland does not have an audit process in which a client instructs a costs lawyer to review their lawyers' work.

As I head towards the end of my legal career, can I suggest my industry look into this service for the Scottish legal market. It clearly needs it!

Issue No 2

To my knowledge, Mr Roddy Dunlop QC (now Dean of Faculty) has not commented on these findings against Mr Brown. This is somewhat surprising, considering our first email exchange in May 2018. See below:

18th May 2018, DUNLOP E-MAIL TO DIAMOND

Mr Diamond

I have been forwarded your email (below). I respond in my capacity as Treasurer of Faculty.

Can I begin my response with a question? In the said capacity, I have been made aware of correspondence from yourself which indicates that a complaint may be about to be made by or on behalf of a client of yours, Mr Bob Kidd, regarding one or more members of Faculty. I am familiar with Mr Kidd, having acted for the defenders in the action which he brought against Paull & Williamsons, although as presently advised I do not consider that this precludes me from answering your queries. Should I understand that the research which you indicate you are undertaking is (a) on behalf of Mr Kidd, and (b) part of a complaint which is contemplated? I ask this purely to understand the context: the answers given below are not dependent on the reason for you posing the questions, but if this is part of a complaint then I may need to account, ultimately, to the SLCC (as discussed further below) in their assessment of how Faculty has handled your complaint. I thus seek clarity in that regard.

Thereafter, you are mainly asking questions of law. Ordinarily we would not answer such questions – you should take your own legal advice. But as these are matters within my ken I answer them. In doing so, insofar as they involve questions of law they provide my own opinion or understanding as to the law. Others may disagree.

- For details of the passage of the Civil Litigation (Expense and Group Proceedings) Bill, see http://www.parliament.scot/parliamentarybusiness/Bills/104998.aspx . The Bill has been passed, though is not yet law (which will require the passing of an Act, as I am sure you are aware). For the passage of a Scottish Bill into an Act, see the explanation athttp://www.parliament.scot/visitandlearn/Education/18641.aspx

- Speculative fee agreements (i.e. agreements whereby a lawyer – whether solicitor or counsel – agrees to act on a "no win, no fee" basis) have been lawful in Scotland for centuries.

- DBAs or contingency fees (i.e. agreements whereby a lawyer – whether solicitor or counsel – agrees to act on the basis that in the event of success (s)he will receive a percentage share of the client's damages) are not presently lawful in Scotland. They will be made lawful by the Bill once it becomes law. Faculty is presently considering whether or not to amend its Guide to Professional Conduct (which presently outlaws DBAs for counsel) in light of the Bill.

- Accordingly any purported DBA prior (at least) to the Act coming into force (and not just pre-1 June 2017) would be unlawful.

- That is not the same, however, as saying (as you do in your email) that "that any arrangement between a Scottish law firm and their client involving additional liabilities/additional fees/success fees pre 1st June 2017 are (sic) unlawful". That would be, to my understanding, incorrect. What is unlawful is a *pactum de quota litis* – i.e. an arrangement whereby the lawyer takes a percentage of any "winnings" in the litigation. An agreement whereby different rates are charged depending on success or failure, or the extent of success, is fairly common, and is not a *pactum de quota litis*. Indeed, on the question of "additional fees", there are express rules of court dealing with same: see *Trunature Ltd v Scotnet (1974) Ltd* 2008 S.L.T. 653.

- Faculty would not purport to consent to any arrangement being entered into between a Scottish law firm and its client. Faculty has no jurisdiction over law firms – only over members of Faculty.

- Faculty would, however, consider any request from a member of Faculty regarding the structure of a fee arrangement proposed by an instructing agent *insofar as that related to counsel's entitlement to be paid*. In the present context, which I understand to be the focus of your question although that is not stated, counsel asked for such approval and was given it – by the then Faculty solicitor who, in turn, had checked this with the then Dean of Faculty (James Wolffe QC).

I note your illustrious career, and your concern. However, I am not sure that either has any relevance to the questions that you pose. I hope that I have answered those questions to your satisfaction. If not, please let me know.

In closing, as I am sure you are aware, if you or your client (whether that is Mr Kidd or anyone else) has a complaint to make about counsel (i.e. any member of the Faculty of Advocates) then the first step would be to complain to counsel him- or herself. In the event of your client not being satisfied by any response from counsel, it would then be open to your client to complain to the Scottish Legal Complaints Commission. Details can be found at https://www.scottishlegalcomplaints.org.uk/

Regards

Roddy Dunlop QC

Treasurer of Faculty.

Diamond e-mail reply to Dunlop

Subject: RE: JIM DIAMOND QUERY ON SCOTTISH LEGAL COSTS

Dear Mr Dunlop,

Thank you again for your e-mail. I am slowly digesting it.

However, in the interim, I wonder if you could send me copies of the letters/e-mails/attendance notes between Mr Brown/Facility Solicitor/James Woolf QC in regard to the funding arrangement?

Dunlop's email to Diamond further replies.

Mr Diamond

You will be familiar with data protection and the incoming GDPR. On what basis do you claim entitlement to see these documents? **And am I to take it that underlying your request is a challenge to the veracity of what I have written?**

If you can clarify these points then I will consider your request.

Roddy Dunlop QC

I could make some BRUTAL comments about the FOA/the above email chain from Dunlop, but I will simply leave it here for others to digest and LOOK to change this system for the benefit of the Scottish people.

One last issue, the former Chairman of Faculty Services, corresponding with me and post-reading an article on billing/rates in FT (featuring my stats on the UK legal market) did e-mail me and suggested

"It might be very interesting to have you talk to members and clerks if you were agreeable".

I always was, as I believe 100 per cent in the VERACITY of my research and knowledge in my field.

The Law Society of Scotland

The LSS decided not to investigate the 14 out of the 15 complaints (which the SLCC stated required considering) against Mr Craik until the litigation was complete. This is even more bizarre when the FOA did not delay their investigation, as mentioned above.

After the litigation, I informed the LSS so they could continue with their investigation. They responded that the matter would be referred to the complaints and oversight sub-committee and decided on in their next meeting on 1 April 2021.

However, the client nor I would be allowed to participate or even be informed of this committee's findings. Below are two examples of the Scottish Law Society (SLS) eligibility decision report against Mr Craik;

Example 1

Issue 10: Mr Craik acted in a dishonest and/or intentionally misleading manner, from around November 2017, in seeking to

create a false narrative that Mr Kidd had received funding for the litigation from a company called Pacific LF Ltd and in making payments to Pacific LF Ltd for which Mr Craik had not properly accounted to Mr Kidd.

DECISION: Issue is accepted for investigation.

In support of this issue of complaint, Mr Diamond has referred to emails sent by Mr Craik to Mr A. In an email dated 1 November 2017, Mr Craik stated:

"... what I would like to do is have the success fee paid to (Pacific LF Ltd) rather than the firm. You are aware of the tax advantages of that. Broadly what I want to show is that the LF company has provided financial support to (Mr Kidd / his company) in the litigation and in return for the success fee, calculated on exactly the same basis as the success fees payable in terms of the letters of engagement. In fact, we have supported the litigation to a substantial extent, you will note that the fees were to be paid monthly and as you know they were not. To give force to the argument that (Pacific LF Ltd) supported the litigation I intend to cross the bulk of the £900k which I hold to fees and then to use that money to make payments to suppliers i.e., counsel."

On 12 November 2017, Mr Craik referred to attached invoices and stated, "these reflect the prior arrangement on how the relationship with (Pacific LF Ltd) works. The first invoice sees (the firm) charging to account of outstanding fees. The second is the outlays invoice as discussed, which LF will pay on (Mr Kidd's) behalf. To be clear LF is 'supporting' the litigation meantime and will be due a repayment in due course".

On 23 February 2018, Mr Craik advised Mr A that he was "working out the invoicing to sort out all fees and give effect to what we agreed yesterday". Mr Craik summarised the funding and invoicing position and stated "Pacific LF have not invoiced so their invoice is £1.89m" adding "Pacific lent £480k to (Mr Kidd) to allow payment of counsel's fees last year so that stands to be repaid with the fee in addition. Total due to Pacific LF, £2,370,000".

Mr Diamond had provided the SLCC with a copy of the Companies House record for Pacific LF Ltd, which shows the company has two directors, Mr Craik and a corporate director called Craik FO Ltd. Based on the information held by Companies House, the SLCC has noted Mr Craik was the sole director of Craik FO Ltd.

Mr Diamond has stated that he received an e-mail from Mr David McKie of the firm on 15 June 2018, in relation to Pacific LF Ltd, which stated "it was agreed some time ago that Pacific LF Limited would assist with cash flow difficulties caused by the client's lack of funds to meet ongoing commitments by paying certain outlays which this firm would otherwise have a liability to pay on the client's behalf".

Mr Macreath has stated that, due to Mr Kidd's failure to make payment of fees which were legitimately due, an agreement was reached that Pacific LF Ltd would meet certain costs which the firm would otherwise be required to meet and, in return, the success fee which would otherwise have been paid to the firm would instead be paid to Pacific LF Ltd. Mr Macreath has stated this arrangement was agreed upon in discussions with Mr Kidd and his representatives and is recorded in writing in e-mails sent with invoices in October/ November 2017. Mr Macreath has stated Mr Kidd took no issue with this approach at that time, because he had approved it.

If Mr Craik acted in a dishonest or intentionally misleading manner with regard to financial accounting in relation to fees and outlays applicable to the firm's handling of Mr Kidd's case, the SLCC considers this could amount to a breach of the Conduct Rules.

The SLCC considers there is limited information available to it at this time with regard to the precise nature of the arrangement referred to in this issue of complaint and how it operated in practice. Based on the information which has been provided, it appears as though the firm held insufficient funds, around November 2017, to pay outlays and take payment of its own fees. Given that the firm appear to have paid some, if not all, of the required outlays around that time, it appears as though a significant amount of the firm's own fees would have remained unpaid. It is unclear what happened at this point; while reference has been made to Pacific LF Ltd having loaned money to Mr Kidd, it appears that this may have been an accounting exercise, rather than an actual transfer of funds from that company.

Mr Diamond has not alleged that this arrangement had any negative financial impact on Mr Kidd, and it does not appear that any interest was charged on the sum referred to as having been loaned to Mr Kidd. With this in mind, it appears the purpose of the arrangement was for the firm to derive some form of tax benefit by facilitating the payment of the success fee plus £480,000 to Pacific LF Ltd rather than the firm's own accounts. While the SLCC considers it is unclear as to whether there was anything unethical about Mr Craik's actions in relation to these accounting matters, it considers his correspondence suggests that the accounting for fees charged by the firm, as well as funds received on behalf of the client, may not have accurately reflected the accurate position. Accordingly, the SLCC considers an investigation of this issue of complaint is required, which may seek to establish whether that was the case and, if so, the reasons for that approach.

For the reasons set out above, the SLCC has determined this issue of complaint is eligible for investigation.

Example 2

DECISION: Issue is accepted for investigation.

Mr Jim Diamond has submitted this complaint on behalf of Mr Robert Kidd and A and E Investments Inc, who were the clients of Mr Craik ("the practitioner") and Levy & McRae Solicitors LLP ("the firm") in relation to the matters being complained about. For ease, reference in this report to Mr Kidd in the context of his capacity as the firm's client can also be referred to A and E Investments Inc. The SLCC has noted that, according to Mr Diamond's own biography, he is "one of the UK's leading experts on legal costs/budgets", with over 30 years' experience in various jurisdictions, including Scotland. Mr Diamond has also stated that he authored "The Tool Kit on Costs Management, "published by the Law Society of England and Wales in 2013.

In relation to this complaint issue, Mr Diamond stated that the firm charged Mr Kidd a base fee of approximately £2.15 million. Mr Diamond has stated that, despite the requests referred to in Issue 5 of this complaint, Mr Kidd has never been provided with the information required to enable Mr Diamond to fully audit the work purportedly carried out on Mr Kidd's behalf by the firm. However, Mr Diamond has noted that, as of November 2016, the firm had estimated their costs as amounting to £899,400 and, having reviewed the work carried out between January 2015 and November 2016, Mr Diamond has stated he has serious reservations with regard to the integrity of that figure.

Mr Diamond has also stated that a law accountant was instructed in relation to this case in July 2017 and produced a report dated 9 August 2017. In his report, the law accountant stated it was unrealistic for him to have reviewed the volume of material the firm had told him existed in relation to the matter, so he had instead only considered the firm's time recording sheets in agreeing that the work undertaken amounted to a total of £899,400. Mr Diamond has advised that he met with this law accountant on 2 October 2018, who admitted he had not actually seen the documents referred to and had instead "rubber-stamped" a draft report produced by the firm. Mr Diamond has also stated that, as the fee figure in November 2016 was stated to be £899,400 from an eventual total of £2.15 million, the remaining fee of £1,250,600 applies to the period from December 2016 to January 2018. He has added that he does not believe much work was undertaken by the firm between December 2016 and March 2017 and, accordingly, the figure of £1,250,600 apparently relates to a period of approximately nine months.

In relation to this complaint, Mr Bill Macreath replied to the SLCC on behalf of Mr Craik and the firm. Mr Macreath stated the position that this issue of complaint had no merit, as the fees charged by the firm had been agreed with Mr Kidd and/or his representatives. He has stated that there is no evidence to suggest the fee charged was "grossly excessive", as alleged by Mr Kidd, and no specification to justify an allegation that the fees charged did not reflect the actual work carried out by the firm. Mr Macreath has also stated that the firm previously offered to provide Mr Kidd with a detailed breakdown of the fee charged, or to submit the file for taxation by the Auditor of Court.

The SLCC has considered the firm's position that the fees charged had been agreed with Mr Kidd and/or his representatives; however, the SLCC does not consider it has been provided with evidence that fully supports this position. While the basis of charging was set out in a Letter of Engagement to Mr Kidd, the SLCC has not seen evidence of such agreement during the course of the transaction and/or at the conclusion of the matter. The SLCC has also considered the firm's position that the SLCC does not have "any jurisdiction on the quantification of fees". While the SLCC does not claim to have a remit to quantify fees in isolation, it can assess evidence provided in relation to such quantification undertaken by other parties.

The SLCC has considered whether it has been provided with sufficient evidence to suggest the fee charged by the firm, in relation to the work purportedly carried out on behalf of Mr Kidd, was not fair and/or reasonable, as required by the Conduct Rules. In relation to complaints of this nature, the SLCC would normally look for such evidence in the form of the outcome of taxation of the relevant files by the Auditor of Court; however, no such taxation has taken place thus far. In the absence of the availability of such evidence at this time, the SLCC has considered what evidence has been provided. In this regard, the SLCC has noted Mr Diamond's experience and views, as referred to above, following his review of the information which the firm has made available to Mr Kidd to this point. The SLCC has also noted that Mr Kidd has raised proceedings against the firm, in the Court of Session, in relation to the fees charged. In the course of those proceedings, the Judge ordained the firm to provide a breakdown of the basic fee charged.

With the above in mind, the SLCC considers it cannot be said there is insufficient evidence to support this issue of complaint and no likelihood of obtaining any such evidence. In addition to the evidence of Mr Diamond, the SLCC considers additional evidence may be available once the present court proceedings have concluded.

For the reasons set out above, the SLCC considers this issue of complaint is eligible for investigation.

As the parties were polarised on the issue of time spent on the case, the matter proceeded to a hearing and on 20 November 2018, Lord Docherty, ordered that Levy & McRae provide a breakdown of the work done.

Let's put this into prospective. Every single UK commercial law firm I have come across over the last 20–30 years have utilised a computer time recording system. Almost all IT systems can record the time spent and include a narrative of the work done. Therefore, from my experience, requesting a breakdown is as simple as being supplied with a copy of the computer time recording of the specific case.

While auditing Levy & McRae's papers and going through approximately 100 correspondence files, I did not find a single computer time record.

Therefore, under the court order, Levy & McRae were required to produce a breakdown of the time spent by the 24 fee earners who worked on the case.

Mr Craik claims to have worked 4479 hours (of which 3012 hrs were under the two headings of 'General' and 'Perusing/Preparing') on this case. This is approximately six hours daily for every working day over three years of the case.

My client as stated above has not been informed of the LSS findings. So, I will repeat again, this was the worst case of overbilling I have ever come across. The case brings shame to the Scottish legal market.

Note:

In October 2021, I was invited by the Scottish Government to take part in a forum on the development of civil costs in Scotland.

I followed this up with an offer to help them pro bono in these developments. I am concerned about the system.

The SLCC is concerned about issues regarding law firms in Scotland. The extract below is taken from their website dated 18 January 2022. The SLCC has raised court proceedings against several firms who have ignored their statutory duty to deliver files on request to the SLCC. Neil Stevenson, Chief Executive, commented,

Our aim in raising these proceedings is to secure the files we need to investigate complaints brought to us. However, it is unsatisfactory that many firms continue to ignore statutory requests that they are legally obliged to meet. This has left us with no choice but to seek the court's support in securing those files.

On the 2nd December 2018, the Sunday Mail ran an article on the case at the start with my headline quote. "Lawyer bill is the most outrageous I've ever seen". This article is still online.

On 3 December 2018, *The Times* newspaper in their Glasgow office published an article titled 'Law firm reported for "Outrageous" bill' in hard copy and online. It followed the Sunday Mail's article. Within a few days, the online version of the article had been pulled and could no longer be found online.

I was curious as to why this article had been pulled but waited until six months after the case was settled to contact *The Times*. I had history with The Times, the London office and specifically their legal reporters. I remember being chased by their former head legal reporter, Ms Francis Gibb, about The Times getting the first call on my hourly rate survey. So, I hoped I had a reputation in my field.

Towards mid-August 2021, I had a telephone discussion with the deputy editor of the Glasgow office of *The Times* about a face-to-face meeting with either him or the journalist who ran the article.

I was due in Glasgow between the 13th and 15th of September 2021 and I chased up the deputy editor on several occasions before travelling up to Glasgow. I received no reply, nothing.

I returned to my contact in The Times London office to see if he could do anything to arrange the meeting with the Glasgow office. Again, I received no reply, nothing.

I sat on this for a month trying to work out what was going on.

In frustration, I issued a data notice request on The Times; after various emails going back and forth with me and four members of The Times legal department, my request was denied. I will leave it to the reader to make their own judgment on why the article in 2018 was pulled by The Times , whilst the Daily Mail article is still live on-line. Fundamentally the same article, both using my quotes. Smell the coffee?

Chapter 16
Trustees' Personal Liability for Legal Costs

My interest in this field of legal costs began while I was working at my first law firm, Baileys Shaw & Gillett (BSG), in the early 1980s. They were well-established and had a reputation for excellence in this field. One of the main clients was Howard De Walden Estates which, to this day, has a vast portfolio of property around central London, including Marylebone High Street and Harley Street. I remember reading the leases provided to the famous doctors of Harley Street at that time. One of the clauses included in the contract was that at no time would there ever be milk bottles left on the steps of the buildings.

Having spent a significant amount of time in Jersey, my interest in the field was further piqued when I came across offshore trusts and the like. I became encompassed by a world of mind-blowing figures from the Abdul Rahman case, which ran for nearly 20 years and took a Jersey judge four years to produce a single judgment, to a more recent case involving the Seigneur of St John, Mr John Dick and his family. The Dicks lived, until recently, in St John's Manor (hence the title), which is often referred to as Jersey's finest house. The case has had tremendous press coverage; there was even a book published about the allegations.

To quote from *The Guardian* in March 2020 (Doward, 2020):

The recent turbulent history of the Dick family reads like a Netflix reboot of Bleak House. For this tale of unending court cases involving the recent sale of a fabulous mansion in one of Britain's better known tax havens, home to a man whose rags to riches life could have been penned by Charles Dickens.

I acted for John Dick's daughter Tanya Dick-Stock in 2018–2019 regarding two legal fee disputes which had run into the hundreds of thousands of pounds.

As I write this book, I am conscious of not using too much legalese. Most of my published articles over the last 25 years follow this trait. However, in 1997 when I was asked to write an article on legal costs for *Trust and Trustees* magazine, which is the leading international journal on trust law and practice (it is the most significant source of information in its field), I spent more time on this article than any other as my source material was huge. I was bringing legal costs issues that had never been published in the 'industry standard'. I remember some long and interesting telephone calls with the editor at the time, John Goldsworth, who was a former barrister of the Middle Temple and held law degrees from the universities of London, Exeter and Cambridge, as well as having a doctorate from Cambridge, regarding the content and various drafts of the article.

I think John was impressed with my one "O" in history no less.

Diana, Princess of Wales

On 31 August 1997, the world witnessed the sad passing of Diana, Princess of Wales. Her passing produced an outpouring of grief of tremendous proportions and resulted in the setting up of a memorial fund in her name.

Setting up these kinds of trusts is a good way to honour the memory of someone with the legacy and popularity of Princess Diana but what people fail to realise is that when you become a trustee of a fund, you can be held personally liable for any financial cost. With this in mind, I wrote to a number of the trustees offering my services to help keep the legal spending under control because I knew there could be a myriad of complications regarding the costs that would be incurred.

Unfortunately, there was no response from anyone. I say, unfortunately, because, over the years, the memorial fund ran into difficulties with reports that at least one-third of the initial funds were spent on legal fees, which included fees for a disastrous legal case involving a US toy manufacturer, which cost the fund millions of pounds.

One report titled 'War over Diana dolls' in *The Evening Standard* on 13 April 2012 referred to the fall-out between Diana's sister and other trustees (Langton and Jobson, 2012). An extract from the article said:

Princess Diana's family were locked in a bitter war of words over a multi-million-pound court battle. Diana's sister Lady Sarah McCorquodale has taken the unprecedented step of strongly criticising lawyers who advised her to sue a US company over protecting Diana's image.

Lady Sarah blames the legal team for advising her to pursue the action against the American firm The Franklin Mint, which produced dolls of the princess. She is poised to give evidence in a dramatic court case scheduled to start in America tomorrow that could cost the Diana, Princess of Wales Memorial Fund millions of pounds.

A *BBC news online* article from 1999 titled 'Diana lawyer resigns from fund' also reported on the fall-out and other issues (BBC news online, 1999):

The chair of the Diana Princess of Wales Memorial Fund has stepped down. Lawyer Anthony Julius had also negotiated Diana's divorce settlement. He will remain a trustee of the fund, which he co-founded in September 1997, soon after the death of the princess in a car crash in Paris.

"I am proud to have been a founding trustee and chair of this fund, which has already committed over £15m in grants and is now set to be a highly effective champion of charitable causes for many years to come, in the name of Diana, Princess of Wales," he said.

Mr Julius' law firm, Mishcon de Reya, caused controversy last year when it charged the fund £500,000 in legal fees. In December, a new law firm took over from Mishcon as legal advisers to the fund.

In an article titled 'Was the £100m Diana Fund a disaster?' dated 21 July 2011 (Pukas and Somerset, 2011), *The Express* newspaper reported on the trust's spending:

Of even greater concern have been the exorbitant sums the fund has shelled out on non-charitable activities. There was the £12,000 spent on Concorde flights – complete with champagne and caviar – for two trustees in 1998 and the £6000 spent on travel by private jet to the Isle of Man the following year. In the first 16 months of its existence £1 in every £3 was spent on legal fees and administrative costs.

The same article also refers to the disastrous US litigation:

The most damaging move by far, however, was the disastrous legal action launched in 1998 against Lynda and Stewart Resnick, owners of Franklin Mint, an American manufacturer of souvenir items.

When the Resnicks produced a Diana bridal doll and commemorative plates the trustees went to court to stop them. They spent £5 million in legal fees – and lost. The Resnicks counter-sued for $25 million for malicious prosecution. Six years later the case was settled out of court with an agreement that the fund would pay the $25 million to a list of charities chosen by the Resnicks.

The article finished with a list of where the fund was distributed.

Where some of the money went:

Children's Investment Fund Foundation – Those living in poverty in developing areas. £2,500,000

Elton John Aids Foundation – Helping sufferers of HIV/AIDS. £2,089,977

Clinton HIV/AIDS Initiative (International AIDS Trust) – Charity aimed at HIV/AIDS and malaria victims. £1,806,904

Landmine Survivors Network – Helps victims and their families to recover. £1,806,904

Rainbow Project – Improving health of gay and bisexual men in Northern Ireland. £301,694

Chinese Mental Health Association – Supporting Chinese people living in Britain suffering from mental health problems. £255,161

Allsorts Youth Project – Project to support young gay people. £220,180

Fairbridge in Scotland – Scottish charity aimed at helping troubled youths suffering from lack of motivation. £187,967

Ethiopian Community Centre – Offering advice and support to Ethiopians living in England. £152,427

Transrural Trust – Aimed at helping women in disadvantaged rural areas. In this case, supporting female beekeepers in Kosovo. £150,300

Roma Support Group – Helps and supports Eastern European Roma Refugees. £143,714

ADFAM National – Providing support for families and prisoners affected by drug use. £78,150

Australian Council on Smoking – Raising awareness of the dangers of smoking. £57,970

I am unsure about the number of people who contributed to the memorial fund. Still, I do not doubt that not one of them made their contribution so the trustees could fly on Concorde while drinking champagne and eating caviar. Also, I doubt if many of them knew that nearly £60,000 was distributed to the Australian Council on Smoking – Raising awareness of the damages of smoking!

The trustees were not the only ones subject to criticism regarding Princess Diana's financial affairs. As *BBC news online* reported on 16 September 1998, the former Prime Minister John Major was reportedly involved in a legal fee dispute with Buckingham Palace regarding Princess Diana's will (BBC news online, 1998). The article stated:

Buckingham Palace has dismissed as a "private family matter" claim that the Royal Princes have been presented with a massive legal bill by their representative John Major.

A British tabloid newspaper reported he ran up a £400,000 legal bill after engaging London-based solicitors Boodle Hatfield to handle the legal work for negotiations over the will of Diana, Princess of Wales.

The former prime minister was appointed in November last year to represent 16-year-old William and Harry, 14, after their mother's death in August 1997.

The boys are due to inherit £12.9m from the estate when they reach the age of 25.

But the bill ballooned when the firm had to sort out legal wrangles over the Diana memorabilia industry and an attempt to avoid death duties, which was later abandoned.

The Palace said: "It is a private family matter. This is something that is entirely for the parties concerned and nobody else."

Mr Major, who does not benefit personally from the charges, has made no comment on the report in The Mirror newspaper.

However, it is understood that he had no idea that the costs were mounting up until he received the final bill. He is then reported to have had it for three months before passing it onto the Palace.

A Boodle Hatfield spokesman said the firm had no comment to make about the unpaid bill.

Original bill £530,000

The current bill only came down to £400,000 after a 30% discount was offered by the company – first 25%, and then after the former Tory leader had hesitated a further 5% was knocked off.

The bulk of the original £530,000 is thought to have come from hiring expert counsel to represent the princes during inheritance negotiations. It is thought that Boodle Hatfield are now pressing for payment and Mr Major has no choice but to pass on the cost to Diana's estate.

During his term in power Mr Major became involved with the royals when he acted as an independent go-between for the Prince of Wales and Diana following their separation.

His appointment as financial guardian came three months after the Princess' death with the approval of the Queen and his successor Prime Minister Tony Blair.

Under his guidance an agreement was quickly reached that the princes' legal bill would be paid from their mother's estate.

It is not for me to comment on the suitability of a former Prime Minster to negotiate legal fees of that magnitude. In his biography, it states that he passed his banking exams. Still, it does not mention what, if any, legal qualifications he received, so I wouldn't be surprised if he was aware of the nuances of, for example, 'The Solicitors Act 1974', which is still fundamentally in place. I wonder if he would have looked for advice from an expert in the field if he had been aware of his possible personal liability. At the time, the 'Solicitors Costs Code 1991' was in place, which stated that a law firm should inform clients of potential legal fees. It was standard practice that if a law firm had to incur substantial expenses on behalf of the client, the client should not only be informed of such but also of the likely costs of the same.

To reiterate, I do not know anything over and above the reports I quoted in this chapter, but I have seen these issues repeatedly rear their ugly head over the many decades I have worked on legal costs disputes.

In 2006 I wrote an article for Society Trust and Estate Planners (STEP), which had over 20,000 members in 80+ countries, following a judgment of the Bailiff of Jersey, Sir Philip Bailhache, in the case of Alhamrani v Russa Management. This case again featured the concept of the trustee's liability for legal costs, but this time in the Jersey Royal Court.

In 2011/12, with the Jackson LJ reforms on civil costs introduced and the emphasis on legal budgets, costs management and proportionality, only one law firm asked me to present a series of seminars on the subject; that firm was Mishcon de Raye. I gave three seminars and gave them my budget software to test internally. They subsequently never used my services, and I have no idea what happened to my budget software.

Chapter 17
The Centre for Policy Studies

The Centre for Policy Studies (CPS) is Britain's leading centre-right think tank. Its mission is to develop a new generation of conservative thinking built around promoting enterprise, ownership and prosperity. The CPS does this by producing its policy papers – particularly on its core areas, tax and cost of living, business and enterprise, housing and welfare. It also works with prominent policy thinkers to bring their ideas to a broader audience, including many Conservative MPs, and hosts events, debates and conferences.

Founded in 1974 by Sir Keith Joseph and Lady Margaret Thatcher, the CPS was responsible for developing the policy agenda known as Thatcherism during the 1980s. Lady Thatcher was quoted as saying, 'The CPS was where our conservative revolution began, and it was by implementing its policies that we gradually restored the confidence and reputation of our country' (CPS, 2022).

In the summer of 2015, the CPS approached me about producing a report about the massive growth of legal fees among commercial law firms. There had been a lot of internal discussion and concern on the topic, and they decided to look into the situation.

I met their former CEO at their offices on Tufton Street, SW1, to discuss the report. Part of the reason for the meeting was that they wanted to evaluate my potential response after the report was published, in terms of whether I would be able to take any criticism which was inevitably going to come my way.

Five minutes into the meeting, the CEO looked at me and said, 'we will not have any problems with you being intimidated by anyone. So, they commissioned me to do the report (for no fee). Over the next six months, I researched and updated my hourly rate survey. I went to my sources and discovered that certain top law firms were now charging their partners £1000 or more per hour. One of my sources said that one firm had hit £1200 an hour for their top partners, which is an astronomical amount. Knowing the press, the way I did, I knew that the £1000 figure would be a huge headline and attention grabber, and the report itself would have a significant impact.

Over the next six months, I had several meetings with the CPS, and the definitive version of the report was ready to be published in February 2016. A few weeks before publication, following a meeting with the CEO, he asked if I had many contacts in the legal press as there was a bit of uncertainty about how the report would be promoted to the mainstream media. In my experience, it was easier to get the mainstream press to reproduce a story once the legal media had published it and given the story or article credibility.

Within seven days of the report being published, there was massive coverage from various publications, including the mainstream and international press. A complete list of media outlets which covered the report can be seen in Appendix 5.

Once the report was published, it was given the most extensive press coverage the CPS has ever received for an external report, both here and overseas. As expected, some responses were critical, and some were brutal.

One example was an article from an online news site titled 'The Report Hating on City Lawyers Is a Load Of Rubbish' (Hamilton, 2016). I suppose I could have gone and confronted the journalist face-to-face. I could have also gone to the two website owners to confront them over the article, but....

Probably the most objective comment came from Dr Catrin Griffiths, editor of *The Lawyer* magazine (Griffiths, 2016):

"UK law firms are utterly useless at collective PR; the public perception of City lawyers stays locked in the 70s. The City of

London Law Society's reaction to the report was lofty to the point of patronising".

I was not mentioned in her article, which I found surprising and disappointing as I had published articles, stats and hourly rate surveys in the Lawyer magazine since May 2001.

Following the publication of the report and the massive press coverage, I was asked to attend a meeting with the Competition and Marketing Authority (CMA) at their offices in Holborn. The CMA wanted to produce a report on the legal marketplace. I met with two investigators and gave a 30-minute presentation about my views on the legal marketplace. Their response to me was, 'we have met numerous people, and no one has mentioned anything like the problems you have just told us about.

I was later invited back in September 2016 to an open debate at their offices with the main legal stakeholders. Everyone was divided into groups and sat at different tables, and the aim was to get feedback on the CMA's initial findings. I was the only individual invited to take part in this forum.

My table included representatives from the Ministry of Justice, Legal Ombudsman and the Law Society. The Law Society's representative pushed for a further five years to bring in the possible changes the CMA suggested. They were concerned that law firms, specifically the small legal practices, would have to invest in IT with budget software which they said was expensive. I pointed out that the Law Society had published a Tool Kit on Costs Management in 2013, which included this software for under £50. The Law Society's representative, taken aback at this, said, 'well, you seem to know a lot about this.

I said "YES"! As I wrote it. The CMA representatives laughed.

With all due respect for the delegates on my table, they simply lacked the working knowledge of what was happening in the real world.

The CMA report was published in December 2016, making damming comments on how law firms lack transparency and suggesting that hourly rates and fees be published on law firms' websites.

Six years later, most commercial law firms still do not publish this information.

Chapter 18
2022 JIM DIAMOND HOURLY RATE SURVEY ("JDHRS")

INTRODUCTION

I have been compiling the JDHRS for over 25 years. It was first published in the 1998 edition of LEGAL500. Subsequent versions have been reported/featured in the legal, national and international press over the last two decades.

In 2016, The Centre for Policy Studies *("Britain's leading centre-right think tank)* published my report "The Price of Legal Services" https://cps.org.uk/research/the-price-of-law/ on hourly rates of the top UK law firms.

The JDHRS was referred to in LSB's Market Impacts of the Legal Services Act, April 2012, The Law Society's Tool Kit on Costs Management, November 2013, and The Law Society's response to the Competition and Marketing Authority's invitation to comment on the market study of legal services in England and Wales, February 2016, the 3rd edition of Friston on Costs 2019 (see over page) and referred to by Judge Davis-White QC, in his judgment in Farmer-v-Candey Ltd Case NO CR-2016-001012 20 October 2019.

The 2022 JDHRS will be my last ever survey.

Research

This is done on an ongoing basis in my day-to-day work and discussions with buyers and sellers of legal services over the last 25 years. I also contacted all top UK law firms with an annual turnover of over £100m and the top 25 US law firms (by The

Lawyer magazine top law firms turnovers) for any input they wished to give.

I started doing the JDHRS in 1998 when after a bad Friday night's sleep, I recall one of my children had colic; I sat in front of my computer at 6 am one Saturday morning thinking this would be a good idea. As clearly, it would be a once-only thing. Not in my wildest dreams did I imagine I'd be doing another one nearly a quarter of a century later.

Over the years, law firms have developed a strategy of publishing their financial figures annually, from turnover to partners' profits, BUT still, they never publish their hourly rates.

Yes, in 2022, it is as hard to find the hourly rates the top UK law firms charge as in 1998. So below is the best information I have collated on the "black arts" of leading UK law firms' hourly rates. So these are guide figures only.

General Comments

1. In 2000 the entire UK law sector's revenue was £8.645 billion

2. In 2021 the entire UK law firm's revenue was £41.6 billion.

3. In 2021 the top 100 UK law firms' revenue was £28.8 billion.

4. As of 26th July 2022, by an article in the Law Society Gazette, 22 law firms have published financial figures for the year.

5. Every one of the 22 law firms has increased turnover. Only one of the law firms with less than a 5% increase in turnover.

6. The two Magic Circle firms that published figures, Clifford Chance and Allen & Overy, increased turnover by 8% and 10%, respectively. With both announcing net profit for the year at 9%.

7. Ashurst announced a 12% increase in revenue to £798m but also reported: "marks a sixth consecutive year of revenue growth – we have now seen revenue grow over 8 per cent on average over the last six years."

8. 2022 therefore, the top 100 UK law firms' revenue reach the £30bn mark for the first time.

Salary Wars

9. 2021/2022 has seen a massive increase in salaries paid, with the NQ (newly qualified) sector specifically seeing astronomic increases with UK law firms trying to keep pace with the US law firms.

10. The Magic Circle law firms are paying £125,000 for NQ lawyers, whereas the US law firms are paying £160,000 for NQ. One US law firm smashes records in the legal marketplace by paying just shy of £180,000.

11. In 2015 the US law firms were paying in the region of £90,000 in comparison to magic circle law firms paying £70,000 for NQs.

12. The simple logic is that these huge salary increases will be passed on to the law firms' respective clients.

13. This is not a criticism of NQs, as the 24/7 work commitment is the price they pay. I wonder how many of them are still in the legal industry in 10 years.

US law firms in the US

It was widely reported in the US media that The United States is objecting to a Johnson & Johnson subsidiary's bid to add Hogan Lovells partner Neal Katyal to its legal team in a high-stakes bankruptcy case, citing his hourly rate of $2,465 — a possible new legal industry high.

1. In an article in Reuters https://www.reuters.com/legal/litigation/jj-bankruptcy-trustee-balks-neal-katyals-2465-hourly-rate-2022-05-23/ 24th May 2022 by Karen Slaon and Mike Scarcella, they stated;

2. *"Partner billing rates at large law firms are considered competitive business information and are typically not public. But they are disclosed in some court filings, especially in bankruptcy cases where a debtor's legal fees must be approved by a judge.*

3. Katyal's hourly rate would rank among the highest publicly available figures in the legal industry. Former U.S. attorney general Eric Holder Jr, a partner at Washington, D.C.-based Covington & Burling, last year billed at $2,295 an hour according to a contract the firm signed with an Oregon university to conduct a workplace culture investigation".

4. **US law firms in London**
   In the matter of <u>Samsung Electronics & Co. Ltd & Ors v LG Display Co. Ltd & Anor</u>, which was widely reported in the legal press in April 2022, US law firm Cleary Gottlieb Steen & Hamilton LLP (London office) had claimed for post eight year qualified lawyer hourly rates at $1,045.00 and $1,475.75. They also argued for 0-4 years qualified lawyer rates at $578.00 and $918.00 per hour.

The **Guideline Hourly Rates (GHR)** were increased on 1st October 2021 with the comparable rates as referred to above at £512.00 (an increase of 25.2%) and £282.00 (a rise of 13.7%). Even with these increases, GHR across the board are nowhere near charging out hourly rates, the rates that clients pay their law firms.

Lord Justice Males, ruling on the costs, said this was 'no justification at all for charging such high amounts. 'If a rate over the guideline rate is to be charged to the paying party, a clear and compelling justification must be provided,' he said.

Counsel

As the Criminal Bar went on strike and picketed outside the courts, the Commercial Bar's fees reached record levels. There are too many variations in hourly rates to include in this survey, but I will have one example of prices commanded by the Commercial Bar.

The irony is that Bar Direct invited me in the early 2000s to discuss the bar's future regarding fees, rates, etc. I was given 10-15mins to present in front of two QCs, one Timothy Dutton QC, the former Chairman of the Bar Council. My presentation lasted about 90mins. I heard nothing until a decade later when I met said QC at a joint client dinner in Mayfair. We chatted generally, and I said I was disappointed that nothing went further, as I believe I had a lot to offer. I also thought the other QC had personally or professionally disliked me. He said he liked the concept and stated that the other QC, who had sadly passed, was taken aback at my views on the Bar's future.

I produced a budget two years ago for one of the UK's most significant ever commercial litigation cases. I discussed with the Counsel's clerk the Brief fees for leading and junior counsel for a trial set for 50 weeks in 2024. The Brief fee includes all the preparation and the first day of the trial; refresher fees are the subsequent days. Figures below:

LEADING COUNSEL   **BRIEF FEE -£5M**   REFRESHER FEES OF £10K PER DAY

JUNIOR COUNSEL   **BRIEF FEE -£3M**   REFRESHER FEES OF £7K PER DAY

These figures and overall legal costs were submitted to the court for a CMC before Mr Justice Baker. Subsequently, my full legal budget was used to assist the 25+ other Defendants in seeking security for costs over £500m.

The subsequent legal costs fall out on this matter can be reviewed in a judgment of Master Leonard on 23rd March 2021 https://www.

bailii.org/cgi-bin/format.cgi?doc=/ew/cases/EWHC/Costs/2021/B11.html&query=(SKAT)

Clinical Negligence

In Jackson LJ's initial report on his proposed changes to the civil justice system in 2009, he quoted hourly rates of over £800.00 per hour in clinical negligence. In 2016, the CPS asked me to assist in a report they had commissioned from Professor Paul Goldsmith on clinical negligence costs. My primary input was looking at costs capping in the US and the comparable spending in the UK & US jurisdictions in this field. My only current reference in this field comes out of a report from the NHS Resolutions annual report 2021/2022

https://www.themdu.com/press-centre/press-releases/clinical-negligence-liabilities-overshadow-public-finances-mdu-warns, which includes the astonishing stats of:

"The report reveals that the change in the discount rate applied to compensation pay-outs caused a 51% increase in current obligations, from £85.2 billion to £128.6 billion".

Professor Goldsmith and others have repeatedly called for the repeal of Section 2(4) of the Law Reform (Personal Injuries) Act 1948. This outdated law requires the courts to disregard the existence of NHS care when determining compensation awards.

CITY OF LONDON (MAGIC CIRCLE) LAW FIRMS

YEAR	NQ-2YRS PQE	5YRS PQE	PARTNER
2003	£175-£185	£245-£280	£375-£450
2005	£180-£215	£250-£300	£425-£525
2007	£235-250	£375-£450	£625-£700
2008	£250	£350-£400	£600-£750

YEAR	NQ-2YRS PQE	5YRS PQE	PARTNER
2009	£250	£375	£450
2010	£300-£350	£450-£550	£650-£725
2013	£350-£425	£450-£550	£700-£850
2015	£350-£500	£500-£575	£775-£850
2022	£450-£600	£650-£850	£1,000-£1500

US LAW FIRMS IN LONDON

YEAR	NQ-2YRS PQE	5YRS PQE	PARTNER
2007	£215-£225	£325-£360	£450-£500
2008	£225	£300-£375	£425-£500
2009	£225	£325	£400
2010	£250-£300	£450-£550	£500-£600
2013	£275-£325	£450-£550	£550-£700
2015	£375-£525	£500-£595	£700-£900
2022	£450-£600	£700-£850	£950-£1350

TOP LONDON LAW FIRMS (OUTSIDE THE MAGIC CIRCLE)

YEAR	NQ-2YRS PQE	5YRS PQE	PARTNER
2003	£150-£155	£215-£225	£325-£375
2005	£175-£195	£225-£300	£350-£475
2007	£185-£225	£285-£315	£400-£495
2008	£195	£250-£295	£375-£495
2009	£180	£250	£375
2010	£180-£345	£285-£535	£375-£640

YEAR	NQ-2YRS PQE	5YRS PQE	PARTNER
2013	£225-£300	£325-£475	£450-£800
2015	£250-£350	£350-£495	£550-£800
2022	£300-£450	£400-£700	£600-£900

Jersey (Top Tier) JERSEY ROYAL COURT in Hard Rock Ltd - v-HRCKY 2013/310 Jersey Royal Court summarily assessed the Defendant's costs at £600 per hour for Partner and £400 for fee earner. The Master stated, "The rate claimed is not so high *to make it unreasonable*".

YEAR	NQ-2YRS PQE	5YRS NQE	PARTNER
2003	£150-£160	£225-235	£300-£350
2005	£175-£215	£235-£275	£325-£400
2007	£195-£225	£260-£295	£400-£500
2009	£275	£300	£475-£500
2011	£285-£325	£300-£350	£400-£475
2013	£285-£325	£300-£375	£400-£475
2015	£285-£350	£325-£395	£495-£625
2022	£285-£350	£350-£450	£550-£725

SCOTLAND

Traditionally seen in the UK as conservative on hourly rates and overall revenue of law firms, for example, Brodies announced in July 2022 a turnover of just under £100m, with this being the 12th consecutive year of growth.

YEAR	NQ-2 YRS PQE	5YEARS NQE	PARTNER
2022	£150-£250	£250-£350	£400-£560

The eye-catching figures, compiled by legal costs expert Jim Diamond, also show that Magic Circle partners' rates have doubled compared to 15 years ago, whilst, according to the Bank of England, inflation has risen 36% over the same 15-year period. Magic Circle partner rates currently sit between £1000-£1500, while US firm partners typically charge between £950-£1350, according to Diamond's figures.

Median hourly rates in London
(Source: Jim Diamond)

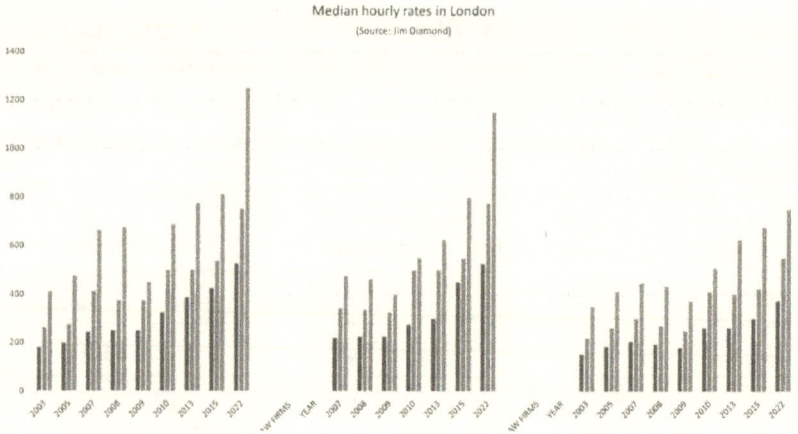

*Courtesy of Legal Cheek

Chapter 19
THE LAST CHAPTER-
"Our Betty" – My Ma

I did a short chapter on my Dad and how his passing had such a life-changing effect on my life. My Mum lived until her late 80s, and I would need a separate book to write about "our Betty", as she was known.

Born in Garston in the 30s, she had ten siblings, and all 13 of them lived in a cramped terraced house in what I suppose was abject poverty. She never talked about her past and was a lost soul when Dad died; she was 49. Her "less is more" in conversations was legendary. Her one-liners could be hilarious and at times brutal.

When I was about 27, I worked in-house for Clifford Turner, had my own flat in London, and had a fab social life, but something was missing. I wanted to run my own legal costs consultancy. I felt that staying at that giant law firm could lead to complacency and a feeling of being institutionalised.

So, a weekend in Liverpool was needed to focus my mind and decide about my future. My mum was to be my soundboard. I chatted with her about the pros and cons of leaving a top law firm with excellent prospects to work independently. She was no one's fool, my mother, very sharp and very direct. Her words of wisdom as she looked at me and said, "*Well, you ain't gonna starve, are you!*" I gave my notice to leave Clifford Turner the following week.

I took a girlfriend to Liverpool for the weekend a few months before. My mum was living on her own and said to me the week before we arrived that she was happy about the two of us sharing a bedroom on the one condition, that I did not tell the neighbours.

The neighbours consisted mostly of people in the 60s, although the house at the end of her road, was the residence of one the most notorious Liverpool crime families.

My Mum phoned me up in or about the mid-90s when she suggested I did not buy the Liverpool Echo that day. It appeared that two members of our family had their crown court trials covered that day in the newspaper. Tentatively, I asked her what they had been charged with, both were up for attempted murder in totally separate cases. It was only because the cases were reported in the paper, that I was even told. To this day, I was never given the facts. A family trait!

I was back in Liverpool about ten years ago, and Mum asked if I could pick up her grandson (my nephew) as his shift was finishing at Tesco's at 10.30 pm. It was about 15 min walk or 5 mins in the car to pick him up. On the way out the door for my uncle "the taxi service", I reminded her that Dad had me collecting money in the late 70s on my own in Liverpool's extremely tough run-down areas. Her reply was, *"Well, your different!"* I laughed as this was one of her legendary one-liners. I picked my nephew up, who was older than I was when I did the collecting money work in the 70s.

Over the years, I would repeat "Our Betty's" one-liners when faced with difficult life or business decisions. *"Well, you ain't gonna starve, are you!"* and *"Well, you're different!"*

And to any working-class kid who is written off, forgotten about and feels worthless. You can, I promise you, make a difference in your own life and maybe others. Lose the anger, lose the chip on one or both shoulders and focus, work hard, and remember- **You Are Different.**

References

Acupay System LLC v Stephenson Harwood LLP [2021] EWHC B11 (Costs).

BBC news online (1998) Palace brushes aside legal bill claims. Available at: http://news.bbc.co.uk/1/hi/uk/172523.stm (date accessed 24/5/2022).

BBC news online (1999) Diana lawyer resigns from fund. Available at: http://news.bbc.co.uk/1/hi/uk/300550.stm (date accessed 24/5/2022).

Bowcott, O. (2016) Ministry of Justice to close 86 courts in England and Wales. Available at: https://www.theguardian.com/law/2016/feb/11/ministry-of-justice-close-86-courts-england-wales (date accessed 24/5/2022).

Brack v Brack (2020) EWHC 2142 (Family).

Brush v Bower Cotton and Bower [1993] All ER 741 (4)

Byrne, M. (ed) (2010) Crunch-busting magic circle ups fees by half. *The Lawyer*.

CPS (2022) Who are we. Available at: https://cps.org.uk/about/ (date accessed 04/06/2022).

Dawkins, M. (2010) Partner rates skyrocket at top firm despite economic gloom. *The Lawyer*.

Doward, J. (2020) Trouble in paradise: Family, feuds and fraud in Jersey. Available at: https://www.theguardian.com/world/2020/mar/15/jersey-dick-family-trouble-in-paradise-offshore-trusts-court-battle (date accessed 24/5/2022).

Francis v Francis and Dickerson [1953].

Goldsmith, P. Prof. (2017) The Medico-Legal Crisis and How to Solve It. Available at: https://cps.org.uk/media/post/2017/the-medico-legal-crisis-and-how-to-solve-it/ (date accessed 24/5/2022).

Gordon, T. (2022) Alex Salmond's QC Gordon Jackson guilty of misconduct for naming sex trial complainers on train. Available at: https://www.heraldscotland.com/politics/20091955.alex-salmonds-qc-gordon-jackson-guilty-misconduct-naming-sex-trial-complainers-train/ (date accessed 24/5/2022).

Gov.UK (2021) Solicitors' guideline hourly rates. Available at: https://www.gov.uk/guidance/solicitors-guideline-hourly-rates (date accessed 24/5/2022).

Greenslade, R. (2011) Diamond takes on lawyers over costs. Available at: https://www.theguardian.com/media/greenslade/2011/sep/26/medialaw (date accessed 24/5/2022).

Griffiths, C. (2016)

Hyde, J. (2016) NHSLA confirms mediation service after pilot success. Available at: https://www.lawgazette.co.uk/news/nhsla-confirms-mediation-service-after-pilot-success/5059084.article (date accessed 24/5/2022).

Hyde, J. (2017) NHS Litigation Authority rebranded to focus on 'early case settlement'. Available at: https://www.lawgazette.co.uk/news/nhs-litigation-authority-rebranded-to-focus-on-early-case-settlement/5060366.article (date accessed 24/5/2022)

Hyde, J. (2022) Judge finds 'no justification' for firm charging £1,100 an hour. Available at: https://www.lawgazette.co.uk/news/judge-finds-no-justification-for-firm-charging-1100-an-hour/5112117.article#:~:text=A%20US%20firm%20which%20tried,the%20case%20in%20competition%20litigation'. (date accessed 24/5/2022).

IBA (2022) About the IBA. Available at: https://www.ibanet.org/About-the-IBA (date accessed 24/5/2022).

Langton, J. and Jobson, R. (2012) War over Diana dolls. Available at: https://www.standard.co.uk/hp/front/war-over-diana-dolls-7226402.html (date accessed 24/5/2022).

Law Society (2015) Increases in court fees will impact access to justice. Available at: https://www.politicshome.com/members/article/increases-in-court-fees-will-impact-access-to-justice (date accessed 24/5/2022).

Optical Services (Jersey) Limited v Carey Olsen [2018] JRC 140A.

McGregor, C. (2017) Whose dime? *In-House Lawyer.* Available at: https://www.inhouselawyer.co.uk/feature/whose-dime/ (date accessed 24/5/2022).

NHSLA (2016) NHS Litigation Authority Annual reports and accounts 2015/16. Available at: https://assets.publishing.service.gov.uk/government/uploads/system/uploads/attachment_data/file/539495/NHSLA_report_2015-16_web.pdf (date accessed 4/6/2022).

NHS Resolution (2021) NHS Resolution Annual report and accounts. Available at: https://resolution.nhs.uk/wp-content/uploads/2021/07/NHS_Resolution_Annual-Report-2021.pdf (date accessed 24/5/2022).

Pukas, A. and Somerset, L. (2011) Was the £100m Diana Fund a disaster? Available at: https://www.express.co.uk/expressyourself/260128/Was-the-100m-Diana-Fund-a-disaster (date accessed 24/5/2022).

QBD and Johnson v Reed [1992] All ER 169.

RE a Company (No 00408010f 1989 (1995) 2 ALL ER 155.

Skilling, M. (2022) Faculty of Advocates tribunal upholds unsatisfactory conduct finding against advocate who failed to inform fellow counsel of success fee. Available at: https://www.scottishlegal.com/articles/faculty-of-advocates-tribunal-upholds-unsatisfactory-conduct-finding-against-advocate-who-failed-to-inform-fellow-counsel-of-success-fee (date accessed 24/5/2022).

SLCC (2022) Further success for SLCC in securing files. Available at: https://scottishlegalcomplaints.org.uk/about-us/news/further-success-for-slcc-in-securing-files/ (date accessed 24/5/2022).

SRA (2019) How we regulate – The Principles. Available at: https://www.sra.org.uk/consumers/who-we-are/sra-regulate/ (date accessed 24/5/2022).

The Lawyer (2021) The Lawyer's top 200 UK law firms revealed. Available at: https://www.thelawyer.com/top-200-uk-law-firms/ (date accessed 04/06/2022).

Wright, J. (2020) Gerry Marsden: 'At 77, it's less funny to be called The Pacemakers – I've got one.' *The Telegraph.* Available at: https://www.telegraph.co.uk/money/fame-fortune/gerry-marsden-77-less-funny-called-pacemakers-got-one/ (date accessed 24/5/2022).

Appendices

Appendix 1 – Sources written by Jim Diamond

(1988) The Paris champions of champions tournament. Black Belt.

(1988) The Paris champions of champions January 1988. Traditional Karate.

(1996) Dinosaur eats lawyer. Legal Costs Journal.

(1997) Trustees personal liability for legal costs. Trusts & Trustee Magazine (3) pp. 11–13.

(1998) Legal costs dilemma (letter). Solicitors Journal. p 980.

(1998) Charge-out rates and billing. Legal 500. pp. 22–23.

(1999) Analysis of a bill: update. Legal 500. p 23.

(2001) Jim Diamond opinion piece. The Lawyer.

(2002) Charge-out rates. Hourly rate survey 2002. Legal 500. p 18.

(2003) Terms and conditions apply. Legal Business.

(2003) Rip-off Britain. Legal Business. pp. 126–127.

(2004) C&I group column. Introduction to Legal Budgets Ltd. p 13.

(2005) Charge-out rates. hourly rate survey 2005. Legal 500. p 15.

(2006) Trustee beware! The Step Journal. p 31.

(2009) Times up. Legal Week.

(2009) Law Works and Jim Diamond press release. Solicitors Pro Bono.

(2012) How law lost its soul – the epidemic of over-charging clients by city law firms. Legal Week.

(2013) Law Society Tool Kit on Costs Management.

(2016) The price of law. Centre For Policy Studies.

(2017) Improving consumer protection and outcomes – latest thinking on quality, pricing, transparency and redress. Westminster Legal Policy Forum Keynote Seminar: Quality assurance and standards in legal services – professional competence, advocacy standards and consumer protection.

(2021) String Theory. The Association of Costs Lawyers.

Appendix 2 – Jim Diamond's contributions at speaker forums/conferences

(1999) IBC UK Conferences Limited. Solicitors' costs after Woolfe. How is the new system working in practice? The changing role of the law costs draftsman.

(2003) Law Society annual conference. Commercial costs: Part 1 – Budgeting.

(2004) IBC 20th Annual Conference. Solicitors costs 2004. A debate – costs budgets and costs capping.

(2004) LexisNexis Professional Education. How to obtain best value from lawyers. (Half-day workshop).

(2005) SCCO Seminar. Costs budgeting; the practitioner's perspective.

(2011) Civil Justice Council. Technical aspects of Jackson implementation expert's workshop.

(2012) Legal week corporate counsel forum conference. Beyond legal advice – turning turbulence into opportunity.

(2013) Jersey Law Society conference.

(2014) The Law Society. Civil Justice Section conference. Cost budgeting – tool kit.

(2016) CMA round table meet of delegates.

Appendix 3 – Sources which have mentioned/ quoted Jim Diamond

Bernal, N. (2015) US firms' UK hourly rates outstrip the magic circle for the first time. *The Lawyer.*

Chellel, K. (2008) Magic circle defies downturn as top billers bump up hourly rates. *The Lawyer.*

Croft, J. (2019) Law firms' love affair with the billable hour is fading. *Financial Times.*

Dawkins, M. (2009) Magic circle hourly rates drop by third as clients flex muscles. *The Lawyer.*

Dawkins, M. (2010) Partner rates skyrocket at top firm despite economic gloom. *The Lawyer.*

Greenslade, R. (2011) Diamond takes on lawyers over costs. *The Guardian.*

Greenslade, R. (2011) Mulcaire's lawyer refuses to say who is paying his legal costs. *The Guardian.*

Heath, I. (2018) Call for independent body to investigate legal costs. *Jersey Evening Post.*

Heath, I. (2015) States failed to control rising Care Inquiry costs. *Jersey Evening Post.*

Heath, I. (2018) Law firm's £60,000 fees slashed by 80 per cent. *Jersey Evening Post.*

Herman, M. and Spence, A. (2010) Top commercial lawyers forced to slash rates. *The Times.*

Kenchington, J. (2009) Magic circle law firms cut fees in half. *City AM.*

Legal Services Board (2012) Market impacts of the legal services act – Interim baseline report.

Malkin, B. (2002) Lawyers remain unpaid after judgment against Tag's CFAs. *The Lawyer.* p 19.

McDonald, C. (2018) Lawyer bill is the most outrageous I've ever seen. *Sunday Mail.*

Miller, L. (2014) Clifford Chance inquiry into FCA 'could cost up to £10m'. *Professional Advisor.*

Peterson, S. (2011) City elite give a little ground on fees but some firms still hiking charge-out rates. *The Lawyer*.

Silvester, N. (2020) Judge savages law firm over £6million bill for tycoon. *The Daily Record*.

Urwin, R. (2008) Hourly rates. *London Evening Standard*.

Waller, M. (2010) No holds barred as price war breaks out in Jersey. *The Times*. p 52.

Williams, M. (2018) 'Disgraceful' £20m cost of Rangers Oldco liquidation leaves creditors with £1.4m. *The Herald*.

(2007) Spiralling hourly rates fail to trickle down to associates' pay packets. *The Lawyer*.

(2007) City high wire act as partners double hourly law fees to £700. *London Evening Standard*. p 30.

(2009) No joke: top firm partner rates falling fast, at least in the UK. *Wall Street Journal*.

(2009) Big firms slash hourly rates. *Costs Lawyer Newsletter* (Issue 6).

(2010) The billing bounce. *The Lawyer*.

(2010) Partners at Magic Circle law firms push rates up. *City AM*.

(2010) City spy: lawyers 'guilty' of jacking up fees. *Evening Standard*.

(2010) Call for investigation as jersey lawyers are accused of 'cartel' style behaviour. *The Lawyer*.

(2011) Channel Islands 'underestimate cost' of LVCR legal case. *BBC News online*.

(2013) Legal costs software. *Insurance Times*.

(2013) Managing costs. A budgeting tool. Software overview. *The Law Society Bookshop catalogue*.

(2018) Law firm reported for 'outrageous' bill. *The Times*.

Appendix 4 – List of media outlets who covered Jim Diamond's report for the CPS

Printed Press

Ames, J and Gibb, F. (2016) £1,000-an-hour lawyers 'restrict access to justice'. *The Times*.

Basham, V. (2016) Report: cost of top London firms restricting access to justice. *The Global Legal Post*.

Bowcott, O. (2016) City law firms charging up to £1,100 an hour. *The Guardian*.

Croft, J. and Fortado, L. (2016) Top London law firm partners charge £1,000 an hour. *Financial Times*.

Doughty, S. (2016) 'Astronomical, unjustifiable': Law firms are slammed for charging up to £1,100-an-HOUR in fees that are restricting access to justice. *Daily Mail*.

Flanagan, M. (2016) Legal eagles feast on fat. *The Scotsman*.

Goodman, J. (2016) Legal tech: easing the pain-points. *Law Society Gazette*.

Goldsmith, J. (2016) Legal fees and the free market. *Law Society Gazette*.

Griffiths, C. (2016) The price is right: how UK firms can steal a march on the Americans. *The Lawyer*.

Hyde, J. (2016) Costs expert slams £1,000 hourly rates at top commercial firms. *Law Society Gazette*.

Hyde, J. (2016) Vara rejects Dyson's description of 'desperate' fees research. *Law Society Gazette*.

Lusher, A. (2016) A legal extortion racket. *The Independent*. (Issue 9) p 1 and p 9.

Kirton, H. (2016) How much does a lawyer cost? Top lawyers' hourly rates are now so high that they're restricting access to justice, as researchers slam the tradition of the billable hour. *City AM*.

Rothwell, R. (2016) Price of Law: are City firms worth their fees? *Law Society Gazette*.

Financial Times: Top London lawyers charge £1,000 an hour, study finds

Financial Times (front page): Top London lawyers charge £1,000 an hour, study finds

Friday newspaper round-up. *IFA magazine.*

(2016) Friday newspaper round-up. *London Southeast.*

(2016) What is the price of law? *New Law Journal* (Issue 7686).

Price of City law restricts access to justice. *Solicitors Journal.*

Article on Lord Justice Jackson and Price of Law. *South Square Digest.*

(2016) Lawyers earning 1,100 pounds an hour put UK justice at risk. *The Business Times.*

A legal extortion racket. *The Independent.*

Top City law firms accused of restricting access to justice by charging up to £1,100 an hour. *The Independent.*

Super-rich clients are distorting the fees charged by lawyers, leaving ordinary citizens without recompense. *The Independent.*

The price is right: how UK firms can steal a march on the Americans. *The Lawyer.*

(2016) Legal eagles in London charging £1,000 an hour. *The Irish Times.*

£1,000-an-hour lawyers 'restrict access to justice'. *The Times.*

The Brief: Research: City law firms bill at £1,000 an hour. *The Times.*

Websites

Aldridge, A. (2016) Magic circle partners bill £110 for typing 'yes' or 'no' and hitting 'send' on an email, claims law firm costs expert https://www.legalcheek.com/2016/02/magic-circle-partners-bill-110-for-typing-yes-or-no-and-hitting-send-on-an-email-claims-law-firm-costs-expert/

Gwyther, M. £1,000 an hour for a lawyer is a fast-cycle rinse https://www.managementtoday.co.uk/1000-hour-lawyer-fast-cycle-rinse/article/1382455

Smith, P. (2016) Top City Law Firms Are Now Charging More Than £1,000 An Hour https://www.buzzfeed.com/patricksmith/city-law-firms-are-now-charging-1000-an-hour?utm_term=.nyVGVaGDw#.hyJx49xRb

(2016) Study says billable hour is unsustainable. https://www.thelaw yermag.com/au/news/general/international-firm-grows-its-asia-pac-team-by-a-fifth/199393

(2016) Top London Lawyers Now Cost More Than £1,000 Per Hour. https://www.bloomberg.com/news/articles/2016-02-05/lawyers-earning-1-100-pounds-an-hour-put-u-k-justice-at-risk

(2016) Lawyers Earning 1,100 Pounds an Hour Put UK Justice at Risk https://www.bloomberg.com/news/articles/2016-02-05/lawyers-earning-1-100-pounds-an-hour-put-u-k-justice-at-risk#:~:text=Cashing%20 in.,or%2018%20pounds%20per%20minute

(2016) Digitallook – Friday newspaper round-up https://www.sharecast. com/news/press-round-up-short-premium/friday-newspaper-round-up-oil-tax-google-sports-direct-hasbromattel--1023253.html

(2016) Lawyers' hourly rates too high for justice. City AM.

Legal Week: The £1,000 question: are City lawyers' rates really too high?

Legal Week: Top law firms charge market rates: why the surprise?

Litigation Futures: Right-wing think tank backs Jackson's call to extend fixed fees

Radio

BBC Radio 4: Today Programme 05/02/2016

Foreign Press

Ansa it Mondo: Parcelle avvocati alle stelle in GB *(Italian)*

Blogo: Avvocati da 1.300 euro all'ora a Londra *(Italian)*

Dagens Nseingsliv: Toppadvokater i London tjener 12.000 kroner timen *(Norwegian)*

Inny Wymiar Codziennosci Weekend: TysiÄ…c funtów za godzinÄ™ pracy (Z CZEGO Å»YJÄ„ LUDZIE) *(Polish)*

Postimees Majandus: Briti advokaatide tunnihind läbistas tuhande naela lae *(Estonian)*

Prawnik.Pl: Astronomiczne stawki prawniczej elity *(Polish)*

RTE: Today in the press *(Ireland)*

Taloussanomat: 1 430 euroa tunnilta – Lontoon lakimiesten palkkiot hirvittävät pienempiä (Finnish)

Kompas.com: Biaya Jasa Pengacara di London Mencapai Rp 21 Juta Per Jam, Bagaimana di Indonesia? (*Indonesian*)

Tribun Lampung: Wow! Sewa Pengacara di Inggris Bisa Rp 21 Jutaan Per Jam! (*Indonesian*)